CAMBRIDGE NATIONAL LEVEL 1/LEVEL 2

Creative iMedia

Student Book

Rich Brooks & Jennie Eyres

CAMBRIDGE
UNIVERSITY PRESS

University Printing House, Cambridge CB2 8BS, United Kingdom

One Liberty Plaza, 20th Floor, New York, NY 10006, USA

477 Williamstown Road, Port Melbourne, VIC 3207, Australia

314–321, 3rd Floor, Plot 3, Splendor Forum, Jasola District Centre, New Delhi – 110025, India

103 Penang Road, #05–06/07, Visioncrest Commercial, Singapore 23846

Cambridge University Press is part of the University of Cambridge.

It furthers the University's mission by disseminating knowledge in the pursuit of education, learning and research at the highest international levels of excellence.

www.cambridge.org
Information on this title: www.cambridge.org/9781009110358

© Cambridge University Press 2022

First published 2022

20 19 18 17 16 15 14 13 12 11 10 9 8 7 6 5 4 3 2 1

Printed in Italy by L.E.G.O S.p.A.

A catalogue record for this publication is available from the British Library

ISBN 978-1-0091-1035-8 Paperback with Digital Access (2 Years)
ISBN 978-1-0091-1432-5 Digital Student Book (2 Years)
ISBN 978-1-0091-1431-8 Digital Learner's Book (1 Year Site Licence)
ISBN 978-1-0091-1433-2 eBook

Additional resources for this publication at www.cambridge.org/go

Cambridge University Press has no responsibility for the persistence or accuracy of URLs for external or third-party internet websites referred to in this publication, and does not guarantee that any content on such websites is, or will remain, accurate or appropriate. Information regarding prices, travel timetables, and other factual information given in this work is correct at the time of first printing but Cambridge University Press does not guarantee the accuracy of such information thereafter.

The teaching content of this resource is endorsed by OCR for use with specification Level1/ Level 2 Cambridge National in Creative iMedia (J834). All references to assessment, including assessment preparation and practice questions of any format/style are the publisher's interpretation of the specification and are not endorsed by OCR. This resource was designed for use with the version of the specification available at the time of publication. However, as specifications are updated over time, there may be contradictions between the resource and the specification, therefore please use the information on the latest specification and Sample Assessment Materials at all times when ensuring students are fully prepared for their assessments. Endorsement indicates that a resource is suitable to support delivery of an OCR specification, but it does not mean that the endorsed resource is the only suitable resource to support delivery, or that it is required or necessary to achieve the qualification. OCR recommends that teachers consider using a range of teaching and learning resources based on their own professional judgement for their students' needs. OCR has not paid for the production of this resource, nor does OCR receive any royalties from its sale. For more information about the endorsement process, please visit the OCR website.

....

....

Contents

Acknowledgements

The authors and publishers acknowledge the following sources of copyright material and are grateful for the permissions granted. While every effort has been made, it has not always been possible to identify the sources of all the material used, or to trace all copyright holders. If any omissions are brought to our notice, we will be happy to include the appropriate acknowledgements on reprinting.

Thanks to the following for permission to reproduce images:

Cover Tara Moore/GI; *Inside* **R093** Stevica Mrdja/GI; Setsukon/GI; Peter Dazeley/GI; Guruxoox/GI; Nico De Pasquale Photography/GI; F8 Archive/Alamy Stock Photo; Koron/GI; Debrocke/Classicstock/GI; Figure 1.4 Logo used with permission of Your Harrogate Radio; Avalon_Studio/GI; JGI/Tom Grill/GI; Alexanderford/GI; Iya Forbes/GI; Geber86/GI; Pekic/GI; Georgeclerk/GI; Ozgur Donmaz/GI; Urbazon/GI; Westend61/GI; Figure 1.12 Museum Buddy (Museum-Buddy.Com); Thomas Barwick/GI; Filadendron/GI; Milko/GI; Dallas And John Heaton/GI; Kelly Bowden/GI; Monty Rakusen/GI; Chris Ryan/GI; Brightstars/GI; Valentinrussanov/GI; Fox/GI; Roman Makhmutov/GI; Cavan Images/GI; Murray Close/GI; Spiffyj/GI; Paul Bradbury/GI; Matteo Colombo/GI; Figure 1.34 Eleanor Grace Twitter: @el.s_artystuff; I Like That One/GI; Klaus Vedfelt/GI; Figure 1.38 © British Board of Film Classification 2021. All rights reserved. Terms and conditions. ™The letters BBFC and the category symbols are registered trademarks of the British Board of Film Classification. (Numbers 2234547-2234552); Figure 1.39 PEGI s.a.; John Eder/GI; Klaus Vedfelt/GI; Thiago Prudêncio/SOPA Images/GI; Valery Matytsin/TASS/GI; Koson Rattanaphan/GI; Homesh Nasre/GI; Mikroman6/GI; Richard Newstead/GI; Chrissteer/GI; Alengo/GI; Eduard Goricev/GI; Sally Anscombe/GI; David Becker/GI; Just_Super/GI; **R094** We Are/GI; Sunwoo Jung/GI; CSA Images/GI; CSA Images/GI; Christopher Furlong/GI; Thomas Barwick/GI; Alexander Spatari/GI; Leon Neal/AFP/GI; Vectortwins/Shutterstock; Onfilm/GI; Cnythzl/GI; Jeffrey Coolidge/GI; Benjamin Knowlson/GI; Figure 2.12 Logo used with permission of Museum of London; Nurphoto/GI; Samad Malik Photography/GI; Image Source/GI; Boris Panov/GI; Cristina Arias/GI; Smartboy10/GI; Mon.na/Shutterstock; Focusstock/GI; Hstrongart/GI; PJF Military Collection/Alamy Stock Photo; Dean Bertoncelj/Shutterstock; Kraphix/GI; Jeff Greenberg/GI; Bounward/GI; Melanie Hagenreiner/GI; Jasmin Merdan/GI; Miragec/GI; Figure 2.36 VectorBitmapExample.svg via Openverse - the original uploader was Darth Stabro at English Wikipedia, licensed under CC BY-SA 3.0; Thomas Barwick/GI; Mint Images/GI; Nata_Zhekova/GI; Chaosamran_Studio/GI; Figure 2.41 'Biomecha' by Laura Watton (PinkAppleJam.com); Figures 2.42 & 2.43 Provided By Rudd Studio; Mediaphotos/GI; Bro Studio/Shutterstock; RLT_Images/GI; Chabybucko/GI; Mikroman6/GI; Mikroman6/GI; We Are/GI; Jasmin Merdan/GI; Tim Grist Photography/GI; Miakievy/GI; grinvalds/GI; Westend61/GI; Yagi Studio/GI

Key: GI = Getty Images

About your Cambridge National Creative iMedia course and qualification

Today's media industry is driven by the creative skills of the people who work in it and the ever-changing technology they have access to. You may want to specialise in one of the many sectors that make up the industry, such as film or advertising, but you will benefit from having experience of a wide range of creative and digital skills.

During your Creative iMedia course, you will learn about the media industry and the tools and techniques that are needed to follow a career in this exciting industry. You'll have a chance to develop skills relevant for a range of roles while developing visual identities for clients, planning and creating original digital graphics and planning, creating and reviewing original digital media products.

How you will be assessed

You have to complete three units.

Mandatory units

- R093: Creative iMedia in the media industry. You will take a written exam for this unit. The exam lasts for 1 hour 30 minutes, and is worth 70 marks. The exam is set and marked by OCR.

- R094: Visual identity and digital graphics. This unit is worth 50 marks. You will be given an assignment with two practical tasks to complete. The assignment is set by OCR and assessed by teachers in your school.

Optional units

You also have to take one of the optional units offered by your school. You will be given an assignment with three practical tasks worth 70 marks for whichever unit you do.

- R095: Characters and comics
- R098: Visual imaging
- R096: Animation with audio
- R099: Digital games
- R097: Interactive digital media

This Student Book covers the two mandatory units: R093 and R094.

How to use this book

Throughout this book, you will notice lots of different features that will help your learning. These are explained below.

These features at the start of each unit give you guidance on the topic area, what you will learn and how you will be assessed.

Thought-provoking questions at the start of units and topics will get you thinking about the subject.

This section gives you information about what content is covered in the topic.

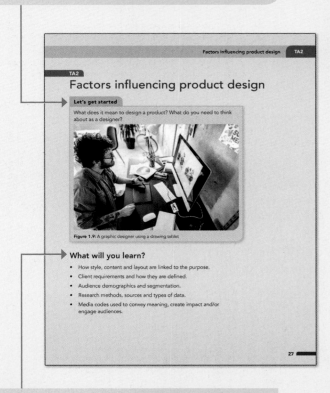

Case studies based on real-life situations put key concepts and practices into context. The accompanying questions check your understanding and challenge you to take your learning further.

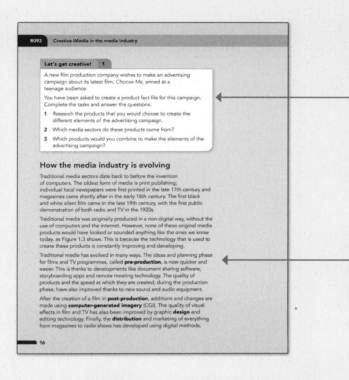

Practical activities that you can do on your own give you the opportunity to practise important skills and techniques, and to prepare for your assessments.

Over to you! activities let you apply your knowledge, and think more deeply about your course.

Key words are highlighted in the text and explained fully in the glossary, often using examples, to ensure you fully understand key terminology.

Stretch 1

Many economy brands use very little white space in their advertising, choosing to show off as many products as possible. High-end brands choose to use a lot of white space on their advertisements.

1 Describe the possible reasons for why high-end brands use more white space on their advertisements than economy brands.

2 Explain why white space is necessary on a digital graphic.

3 Analyse the impact both poor and effective use of white space can have on a digital graphic.

Stretch activities and questions give you the opportunity to try more challenging questions and to extend your knowledge.

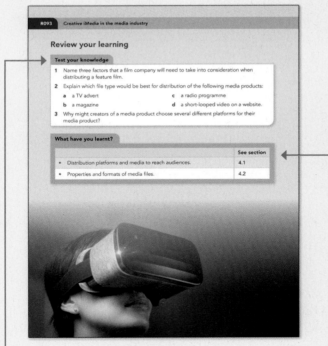

These question boxes give you regular opportunities to test your knowledge so that you feel ready for your exam or assessment.

Summary sections help you review your learning, to check you understand key concepts and can apply your learning. They also show you where to look back for more information if you need to read it again.

Support for you

Whilst all three of the following components can be used separately, they have been designed to work together, to provide comprehensive support for your Cambridge Nationals course.

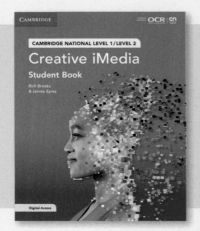

Your Student Book covers all the mandatory units and is where you will find the core information you need. This will help you with your knowledge and understanding of the subject. Information is arranged by unit and then by topic area, so you can easily find what you're looking for. Questions and activities will help you to apply your knowledge and understanding and to develop practical skills. You can assess your progress with the Test Your Knowledge questions. When you've completed the quiz, check your answers in the digital edition.

Your Revision Guide and Workbook supports you with the externally assessed unit of your course. The exam preparation section offers advice to help you get ready for this assessment. The revision guide section provides concise outlines of the core knowledge you need. Each page focuses on a small piece of learning to help you break your revision up into manageable chunks. The workbook section brings your revision and learning together with practice questions. Digital quizzes help you to understand the language used in your assessment and to check your knowledge and understanding of key concepts. The Revision Guide and Workbook has not been through the OCR endorsement process.

The Teacher's Resource covers all the mandatory and optional units and is a rich bank of ideas to help your teacher create engaging lessons to meet the needs of your class. It contains PowerPoint slides, worksheets and audio-visual material, in addition to activity and delivery ideas that can be personalised for your lessons. Digital quizzes help test understanding and unlock the language used in assessment.

R093 Creative iMedia in the media industry

Let's get started

Media refers to ways of communicating to large groups of people. What do you think we mean by 'the media industry'? What sectors are there in the media industry?

Which sector of the media industry would you like to work in?

What will you learn in this unit?

Creators of adverts, films, websites and other media products do not work on their own. They work as part of the media industry. This industry has many different sectors. It is made up of national and global companies, as well as individuals and small teams of creative designers and media producers. There are many job roles available in the media industry. In this unit you will learn about these job roles and the responsibilities of the individuals in these roles.

The creation of media products is the main function of the media industry. In this unit you will find out about the planning, design, creation and distribution of media products for a variety of audiences. You will also learn about the legal and ethical issues that affect the industry.

In this unit you will learn about:

- the media industry **TA1**
- factors influencing product design **TA2**
- pre-production planning **TA3**
- distribution considerations **TA4**.

How you will be assessed

This unit is assessed by a 90-minute exam with 70 marks that is worth 40 per cent of your overall mark. In the exam, you will be expected to show that you understand this unit by recalling some media industry knowledge, applying your knowledge by responding to a brief and using your analysis and evaluation skills.

The media industry

Let's get started

Which industry sector(s) do you think the BBC fits into?
What media products does the BBC make?

Figure 1.1: BBC Television Centre in London is still an iconic building where filming often takes place

What will you learn?

- Media industry sectors and products.
- Job roles in the media industry.

1.1 Media industry sectors and products

The word 'media' can describe different forms of communication, or products that communicate a message to us. All the different forms of communication, products and the companies that make the different products sit within different sectors (groups) of the **media industry**.

The media industry dates back to the late 17th century. Since then it has been constantly evolving, as new technology has been developed. There was a huge change in the late 20th century when technology, and therefore many areas of the media industry, became digital. Using digital technology, media products could be created using electronic tools and systems, including computers and the internet.

Sectors of the media industry

There are many different types of company in the media industry. There are small-scale local or national companies that often focus on one type of media product only. They may well have just a few people working for them, and those individuals may perform a variety of job roles spanning more than one **production** phase (see 'Production phases' at the end of this section). Examples of small-scale media companies include Coffee Films, Ustwo Games, *American Chordata* magazine and The Firm music production house.

At the other end of the scale, there are huge multinational, or even global, companies producing many different types of media products. These large-scale companies often have thousands of employees, each with a very specific job role. Examples of large-scale media companies include Channel 4, Facebook, EA Games, News Corp and Warner Bros.

The media industry can be broken down into two types of sectors, based on the kind of media products they produce: traditional media sectors and new media sectors. As Figure 1.2 shows, there are four main traditional media sectors and four main new media sectors.

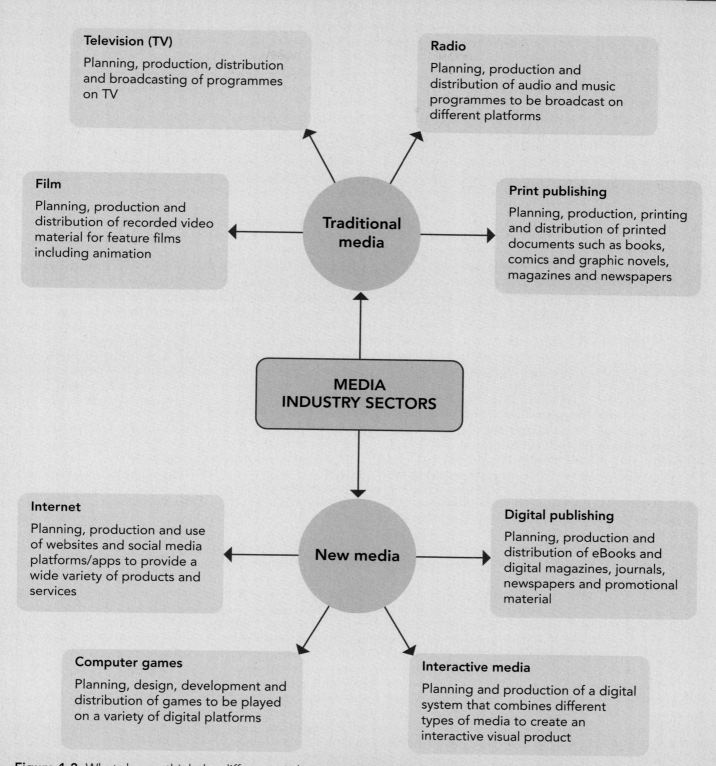

Television (TV)
Planning, production, distribution and broadcasting of programmes on TV

Radio
Planning, production and distribution of audio and music programmes to be broadcast on different platforms

Film
Planning, production and distribution of recorded video material for feature films including animation

Traditional media

Print publishing
Planning, production, printing and distribution of printed documents such as books, comics and graphic novels, magazines and newspapers

MEDIA INDUSTRY SECTORS

Internet
Planning, production and use of websites and social media platforms/apps to provide a wide variety of products and services

New media

Digital publishing
Planning, production and distribution of eBooks and digital magazines, journals, newspapers and promotional material

Computer games
Planning, design, development and distribution of games to be played on a variety of digital platforms

Interactive media
Planning and production of a digital system that combines different types of media to create an interactive visual product

Figure 1.2: What do you think the difference is between traditional media and new media?

Products in the media industry

Many different products are created and used by media industry sectors. In fact, the same media product can be used by multiple different sectors. Media products can also be combined in order to meet the needs of their **target audience**. The target audience is the group or groups of people at which the product is aimed. Table 1.1 shows the different types of products and the sectors within the media industry that use these products.

Table 1.1: Think of a media product you have used recently. What other media products may have been used to create it?

Name and description of product	Sectors that may use these products		Examples
	Traditional	**New**	
Video: Recording, editing and production of moving visual images	Film, TV	Computer games, interactive media, internet	Film, TV programme, advert, video game cutscene, trailer
Audio: Recording, editing and production of vocal and/or other sounds or noises	Film, TV, radio	Internet, computer games, interactive media, eBooks	Radio programme, podcast, soundscape, advert, audiobook
Music: Recording, arrangement and production of vocal and/or instrumental sounds	Film, TV, radio	Internet, computer games, interactive media	Jingle, soundtrack, music video, TV intro/outro, underscoring
Animation: Digital photographing or computer generation of drawings or models to create the illusion of movement	Film, TV	Computer games, internet, interactive media	Advert, film, TV programme, phone app, animated banners
Special effects (SFX): An illusion created by props, camerawork or lighting	Film, TV	Computer games	Models, pyrotechnics, green screen, text overlays
Visual effects (VFX): Computer-generated imagery to enhance a video recording			
Digital imaging and graphics: Creation of pictures or designs using digital software, a digital camera or scanner	Film, TV, print publishing	Internet, computer games, interactive media, digital publishing	Book covers, billboards, logos, van wraps, album artwork, magazines, web graphics
Social media platforms/apps: Digital-based programmes that encourage connections and communication between their users, using the internet and digital devices	Film, TV, radio	Computer games, internet, interactive media	Facebook, Instagram, TikTok, Twitter, LinkedIn, TuneIn, BBC Sounds
Digital games: Games that are played using digital technology		Computer games, internet, interactive media	For web, mobile phone and tablet, PC, games console

Table 1.1: Continued

Name and description of product	Sectors that may use these products		Examples
	Traditional	**New**	
Comics and graphic novels: Stories that are told using pictures in panels, along with text and speech bubbles	Print publishing	Digital publishing, internet	Manga comics, superhero graphic novels, children's comics, children's graphic novels
Websites: Collections of web pages containing text, images and interactive elements	Film, TV, radio, print publishing	Digital publishing, internet, computer games	Informational, e-commerce, blogs, social media, directories, promotional, entertainment
Multimedia: Combines different types of media into one presentation or form of communication	Film	Computer games, internet, interactive media	Information kiosks, presentations, interactive DVD extras
eBooks: Digital versions of printed books that can be read on a device such as a computer, phone or tablet		Internet, digital publishing, computer games, interactive media	Fiction, instruction booklets, guides, handbooks, walk-through
Augmented reality (AR): When computer-generated images on a screen are combined with a real-world environment	Film	Computer games, interactive media	Video games, YouTube videos, Google search, immersive education, simulation
Virtual reality (VR): Computer-generated sounds and images that are not part of the user's real-world environment			

Over to you!   1

These examples show where media products are combined:

- A **computer game** combines digital game, video, animation, special effects, digital imaging, music and audio products.

- An **eBook** combines digital publishing, digital imaging and graphics, the internet and even interactive media products.

Can you think of another example of a media product that combines different products? Use Table 1.1 to help you.

Let's get creative!   1

A new film production company wishes to make an advertising campaign about its latest film, *Choose Me*, aimed at a teenage audience.

You have been asked to create a product fact file for this campaign. Complete the tasks and answer the questions.

1   Research the products that you would choose to create the different elements of the advertising campaign.

2   Which media sectors do these products come from?

3   Which products would you combine to make the elements of the advertising campaign?

How the media industry is evolving

Traditional media sectors date back to before the invention of computers. The oldest form of media is print publishing; individual local newspapers were first printed in the late 17th century and magazines came shortly after in the early 18th century. The first black and white silent film came in the late 19th century, with the first public demonstration of both radio and TV in the 1920s.

Traditional media was originally produced in a non-digital way, without the use of computers and the internet. However, none of these original media products would have looked or sounded anything like the ones we know today, as Figure 1.3 shows. This is because the technology that is used to create these products is constantly improving and developing.

Traditional media has evolved in many ways. The ideas and planning phase for films and TV programmes, called **pre-production**, is now quicker and easier. This is thanks to developments like document sharing software, storyboarding apps and remote meeting technology. The quality of products and the speed at which they are created, during the production phase, have also improved thanks to new sound and audio equipment.

After the creation of a film in **post-production**, additions and changes are made using **computer-generated imagery** (CGI). The quality of visual effects in film and TV has also been improved by graphic **design** and editing technology. Finally, the **distribution** and marketing of everything from magazines to radio shows has developed using digital methods,

Figure 1.3: Why not ask someone aged 40+ to tell you about cassettes, video tapes and floppy disks? They may even be able to show you some real-life examples

such as streaming and web advertising so products have been able to reach new audiences.

New media sectors are those which have evolved due to the invention of computers and the internet. New media sectors are always evolving because the digital technology they are produced with and accessed on is constantly improving. Many types of digital technology have now come together on a single device/platform. For example, tablets and phones allow audiences to access a range of different types of new and traditional media from one device. This is **technological convergence**. It has led to larger numbers of consumers, who can access a wide variety of media products in more ways than ever before.

Over to you! **2**

1   Make a list of the many different media products you can access from your phone.

2   Write down how you would have accessed these different types of traditional and new media products before technological convergence. For example, film – in the cinema or on a DVD player.

3   How do you think technology will further converge in the future?

Case study

Your Harrogate radio station

North Yorkshire-based radio station Your Harrogate Radio was set up in March 2021 by Adam Daniel and Nick Hancock. Nick had previously presented on Stray FM, an independent radio station that played on different platforms and served the local area. Stray FM was taken over by the Greatest Hits radio network, owned

Figure 1.4: Your Harrogate Radio offers local information and community news

and operated by the global company Bauer Media Group. It was renamed Greatest Hits Radio (Harrogate and the Yorkshire Dales) and no longer had the same local feel to it. Adam and Nick realised that there was still a strong desire for a local radio station. So they came up with Your Harrogate Radio.

Before digital radio came along, radio stations were only broadcast using AM, FM and LW radio waves. Listeners had to have a physical radio tuned into the correct frequency. Radio station operators also had to buy expensive **licences**, costing thousands of pounds a month. A small, independent station like Your Harrogate Radio would have struggled to buy such an expensive licence and would have been competing with much larger companies.

Your Harrogate Radio has been able to utilise digital technology to form an internet-only radio station that can broadcast to anyone, anywhere without the need for tuning or worrying about the strength of the radio signal. This is also a much more affordable radio model as no licence is needed to broadcast over the internet, just for the music being played. Audiences can now listen to the station online via their website, on a smart speaker (such as Amazon Echo or Google Nest), on DAB digital radio and on the Your Harrogate Radio app. This means that audiences can listen on their smartphone or tablet whilst on the move.

Continued

Despite being an internet-only product, Your Harrogate Radio is advertised using traditional media (such as flyers, magazine adverts and billboards), as well as new media (such as web page and social media digital advertising).

Check your understanding

1   What is the difference between traditional broadcast radio and internet-only radio?

2   There are clear benefits for both producers and audiences of internet-only radio. What are these benefits?

3   Explain why it is important for Your Harrogate Radio to use traditional media and new media products to advertise the station.

Production phases

All media products follow the same creation journey, whether they are forms of traditional media or new media. Each media product journey starts with an idea, which is developed into a **concept design**, goes through the pre-production and production phases and ends with distribution. Figure 1.5 shows this journey in phases.

Phase 1 **Pre-production**	• Products are researched • Ideas and concepts are developed, planned and designed (concept design)
Phase 2 **Production**	• Product parts are created from the designs • They are created by people and organisations called producers or creatives
Phase 3 **Post-production**	• All the parts are brought together • They are edited to form a final product
Phase 4 **Distribution**	• Products are sent out in different ways for audiences to access • This often happens on a range of platforms

Figure 1.5: Do you think these phases always happen one after another?

1.2 Job roles in the media industry

Job roles in the media industry can be split into three different areas: creative, technical and senior.

Creative roles

If you are in a creative role, your job will be to come up with and develop ideas to help create a product for the target audience. You would generally be needed in the pre-production and production phases.

Figure 1.6: This is one way of generating 3D characters for video games. What are the others?

- **Animator:** An artist who draws or creates images, called frames, that are put next to each other to create an animation. An animator would be given a storyline or brief to create the frames from.

- **Content creator:** Generates ideas, messages and information for target audiences from a brief given to them for the product by the **client**.

- **Copy writer:** Writes clear, interesting text to educate, sell to or engage audiences. For example, this could be text on a website or in a digital magazine.

- **Graphic designer:** With the aid of computer software, they create and put together graphics using fonts, images, photos, illustrations and shapes. These graphics could be used to form part of a larger product, such as a website, or could form the whole product, such as a film poster.

- **Illustrator/graphic artist:** An artist who draws freehand digital or physical artwork to be used in a graphic or other media product. This artwork will be used alongside other elements such as text or photographs.

- **Script writer:** Creates written text that forms the dialogue and sound for a media product, allocating it to characters within the storyline. A script may be used alongside a range of visual elements or may be used for audio only.

- **Web designer:** Plans and creates web pages and sites using interactive features, for example sound, graphics, video and text. These web pages are then combined to form a website.

- **Photographer:** Captures and edits images of people, places, events and objects. These could be used to enhance media products, or could be the main focus, such as on the cover of a magazine.

Figure 1.7: This photographer is working in a studio. How can you tell?

Technical roles

If you are in a technical role, you will be using technology and operating equipment to develop, improve and finalise media products. You would generally be needed in the production and post-production phases.

- **Camera operator:** Uses camera technology to film video footage as part of a crew. Often works from a storyboard and takes direction from the director as to which shot types and angles should be used.

- **Games programmer/developer:** Uses coding to build and test parts of a computer game.

- **Sound editor:** Chooses, edits and puts together sound recordings that have been created by the audio technician and voice actors. This is often done after the video footage has been created, to enhance it.

- **Audio technician:** Sets up and uses audio equipment to record sounds which will then be edited by the sound editor.

- **Video editor:** Chooses, edits and puts together video recordings, alongside the sound editor.

- **Web developer:** A programmer who creates web pages and websites using code. The media products made by the creatives will be incorporated into the website at this stage.

Figure 1.8: This camera operator is using a shoulder mount. How does this affect the footage taken?

Senior roles

If you take on a senior role, then you will oversee the creation and development of products and projects. You will support and manage some or all of the technical and creative roles. You will therefore be needed in the pre-production, production and post-production phases. You will also oversee the distribution of the final product.

- **Campaign manager:** Creates and runs marketing and advertising projects for products once they are almost ready to be distributed. Often, the product is not yet finished, but the marketing and advertising campaign will already have started so consumers will buy it as soon as it is distributed.

- **Creative director:** The head of a team that creates a plan or strategy for the creative development of a product. This plan would be clear from the concept design in the pre-production phase and would run right the way through. The creative director would be responsible for the success of the plan.

- **Director:** Communicates with the client, leads the project and distributes tasks to other members of the team for them to complete. A film director would lead and direct the cast and the crew, assigning different tasks and responsibilities to them when on set.

- **Editor:** In charge of refining and checking the product, they make sure it performs as well as it can – technically, artistically and for its target audience. A newspaper editor would make sure that the newspaper content is accurate, that it looks professional and is in line with previous editions.

- **Production manager:** Organises budgets, production schedules, the cast and crew, as well as locations and other practical elements at each stage of the project. This role focuses on the smooth running of all parts of the project, from start to finish.

Let's get creative!   2

Choose any recent film, TV programme or computer game to make a presentation about.

Carry out some research into how and when it was made. Try to find information about the phases of production and the job roles and responsibilities involved in creating this media product.

1   Create a timeline of the production phases for your product that match the media industry phases. Label the timeline with appropriate job roles for each phase.

2   Visit the ScreenSkills website, or another suitable website. Search for the job roles you have identified to learn more about the responsibilities of these roles and make notes.

3   Apply your knowledge of job roles, along with your research, to discuss what responsibilities you think each of the job roles involves.

Responsibilities

Each job role has responsibilities and contributes to the development of a product or project, in one or more of the different production phases.

Table 1.2: Which of these responsibilities do you think would be the most difficult to take on?

Creative role responsibilities
• Prepare drafts and models of product ideas for review by clients
• Communicate ideas to other members of the creative team
• Tailor ideas to ensure target audience needs are met
• Research target audience and competitor products
• Work alongside other creative, technical and senior colleagues as part of a team
• Create visually appealing or interesting media content
• Develop creative ideas following feedback
• Work with other creatives to come up with and develop ideas
• Meet production deadlines for creative content
• Liaise with clients about production of products and address feedback
• Ensure that client requirements of the brief are met
• Produce professional, original media content which meets client requirements
• Produce and select creative ideas for media products
• Use specialist software to create media products

Table 1.3: Are there any responsibilities here that you would enjoy?

Technical role responsibilities
• Communicate with lighting and sound specialists
• Work closely with creatives to produce media content
• Create tests to check that media products work
• Use technical equipment correctly to create media content
• Assemble and set up equipment correctly to produce media content
• Find technical solutions through problem-solving
• Practise using and testing media production equipment
• Repair and maintain media production equipment
• Use specialist software for production of media content
• Follow scripts, storyboards and visualisation diagrams to produce media content
• Advise on the best way to create a media product and what equipment to use
• Work alongside other technical, creative and senior colleagues as part of a team
• Mix and balance assets to ensure the quality of media products

Table 1.4: Which of these responsibilities do you think happen in which production phase?

Senior role responsibilities
• Set quality control procedures in place
• Give advice and guidance to creative and technical colleagues
• Evaluate success of products and projects
• Formulate and run projects or campaigns
• Manage a team of creative and technical colleagues
• Understand the target audience and market
• Decide how to promote and market media products
• Motivate a team of creative and technical colleagues
• Make sure the final product of a media project meets client requirements
• Liaise with the clients about projects
• Manage media project budgets
• Supervise all stages of media projects
• Hire and brief technical and creative colleagues
• Ensure that health and safety regulations are met
• Monitor progress of media projects and report to clients

Stretch

You have been given the role of production manager for a new documentary set behind the scenes in the animation industry. It is aimed at children aged 8–12 and will contain some original animations, as well as interviews and 'fly on the wall' footage. You will need to create a strong team to run this project successfully.

Which creative, technical and senior roles will you need to include to ensure the project runs smoothly, during each production phase? Justify your choices.

Multiple roles

Media job roles are not always completely independent from each other. Sometimes the size of company or the scale of a project means that one person takes on more than one role. They will have responsibilities in several areas.

A small company may have the same person in more than one creative role, or both a creative and a technical role. In some cases, those working in senior roles also get 'hands on' and complete creative or technical roles as well. This would be particularly likely if the individual in a senior role had worked in that creative or technical role previously.

If a company or organisation is very large, one person may take on the same creative, technical or senior role for many different projects at the same time. For example, an editor may edit more than one publication. This may be called 'multi-tasking'.

It is likely that if an individual is working in more than one job role (creative, technical or senior) they will be involved in more than one of the production phases of a project.

Review your learning

Test your knowledge

1 For each of the products below, identify what media sectors they come from.

   a A fiction book in paperback and an eBook

   b A new video app on which friends can make videos and share them

   c An animation for a new web advert

2 Explain which job roles would be needed to create each of these products and why.

What have you learnt?

	See section
• Media industry sectors and products.	1.1
• Job roles in the media industry.	1.2

Factors influencing product design

Let's get started

What does it mean to design a product? What do you need to think about as a designer?

Figure 1.9: A graphic designer using a drawing tablet

What will you learn?

- How style, content and layout are linked to the purpose.

- Client requirements and how they are defined.

- Audience demographics and segmentation.

- Research methods, sources and types of data.

- Media codes used to convey meaning, create impact and/or engage audiences.

2.1 How style, content and layout are linked to the purpose

Purpose

Media products are created to do a particular job for a particular audience. There is always a reason for a product's creation, and this is called its **purpose**. Sometimes a media product may have more than one purpose as it may be trying to evoke different responses and emotions in different people. The five main purposes of media products are detailed in Table 1.5.

Table 1.5: The main purposes of media products

Purpose	Description	Examples
Advertise/ promote	To advertise or promote a physical product, service, organisation or idea	Billboard, radio advert, web banner, film poster, flyer, TV advert, magazine or newspaper advert
Educate	To teach or provide instructions for someone to learn something	Textbook, leaflet, webinar, website, podcast, instruction manual, 'How to' guide, app, documentary
Entertain	To provoke an emotional response, for enjoyment or to provide escapism from daily life	Comic, magazine, TV programme, film, radio programme, social media, podcast, video game, music video
Inform	To give brief instructions or information without going into depth	Map, flyer, poster, booklet, website, social media, instructional video, sign, digital report, news programme
Influence	To have a persuasive effect on an audience to make a choice, or to change or inform their view	Social media, music video, charity animation, podcast, party political broadcast

When a designer or creative team receives a **client brief**, they will need to work out the purpose of the media product before they can do anything else. If a product is intended to inform, this will need a very different approach to one which is intended to advertise. In Figure 1.10, for example, you can see two bus stop posters, with very different purposes. The purpose affects the style, content and layout of each poster even though they may have potentially overlapping target audiences.

Figure 1.10: What do you think is the purpose of each poster? How do you think the purpose of the poster may affect the way it looks?

Style, content and layout

To come up with an effective design idea, there are three important elements that you need to consider. These are style, content and layout, and they all combine to form a cohesive product idea. All these elements are then adapted to meet the purpose of the media product, as well as the potential target audience.

Style

Style is the combining of colours and themes to create an overall feel or look for a media product. This combination brings together requirements of the client brief, elements of appearance from the content of the product, along with what is currently popular or trending, and target audience demands.

Style can also relate to the way audio or video content is represented or expressed. Choice and selection of footage and images is important here, along with sound, lighting, props, costumes and text fonts that would all need to be adapted to meet the required purpose.

The purpose of a hip-hop music video, for example, is to entertain its target audience. The purpose of a school open day video would be to inform and persuade its target audience, therefore sound and visuals will be presented in a very different way in each of these products. The music video may be studio-based and use dark backgrounds, graffiti, metallic and bright neon colours, whereas the open day video may be set in locations around the school with natural lighting and pale colours to demonstrate a welcoming style.

Figure 1.11: Both images have very specific styles – what tone or feeling has been created by these styles?

One example of using style is in a children's comic. The comic will need a colour scheme that relates to the message the client wants to get across and fits with the purpose of the magazine, which is to entertain. As a designer you might choose bright colours, along with interesting and bold fonts. The title of the comic will also be important and will influence the style, along with the age group of the audience and what their current interests are.

Content

Content is the message and experiences within a product that the client wishes to convey. The creative team needs to know what the media product should be about, and the message that the client wants to express to the target audience. In a film, this is likely to be the plot or storyline, in advertising this could instead be a product or a concept. The content should be clear from the start, and is adapted to meet the specific purpose.

The content you design and create will represent the message in a particular way dependent on how it is created. For example, if the content and purpose of a podcast is educational children's adventure stories, there will be a range of appropriate audio selected. One sound may be a narrator with a friendly and interesting voice, another could be catchy sound effects suitable not just for the age group, but for the educational purpose and the genre of stories too.

Dependent on the purpose, either formal or informal language could be used to convey the message through the content. A short documentary film would use much more formal language than a radio comedy show, and a textbook would use more formal language than a social media app. The tone of language is also important; this could be anything from friendly and inviting to angry or serious dependent on the purpose and the client requirements.

INTERACTIVE MAPS
Easy-to-use maps. Helps you zip through the numerous rooms at the museum without getting lost.

INFORMATIVE
Informative and interesting commentaries. Not too long. Not too short. Just right!

EASY SEARCH
Find your favourite artefacts easily. Spend time browsing & not in walking!

SELF-PACED TOURS
Make the best use of your limited time. Be it 1 hour, two hours or the whole day.

Figure 1.12: What do you think an interactive multimedia app like this adds to the museum experience?

An example of content could be the rooms in a museum and the exhibits within them. The client may want to try to bring the museum to life in a virtual way by creating an interactive phone app showing all the exhibits so that families can interact with them. The purpose of this app, therefore, is to inform, educate and entertain.

Layout

The way you structure or arrange a product, and the positioning of the elements, is called the layout. The layout is dependent on the size and shape the product needs to be, along with the elements that need to be included and their arrangement. Some of the key elements that may be needed include product image, product name, and images of main characters.

There are also expected **conventions** for each media product. A convention is a predictable set of components that the audience would expect to see in a product, having been established by all the media products that have gone before it over time. Conventions can relate to genre (for example, science fiction, western or comedy) or form (for example, poster, mobile phone app or website). The purpose of a media product would directly influence the form and therefore layout of a product.

The conventions of a newspaper are: black text printed onto paper that is longer than it is wide; a large heading or title on the front (called a masthead) which carries the name of the newspaper; and each page is set up in columns with a series of short articles on each page with pictures.

If the purpose of the newspaper is to inform and educate then it's unlikely there will be lots of colour and there will only be a limited number of photos and graphics. The focus will be on the text and making sure it is factually accurate. If entertainment is an additional purpose of a newspaper then you could expect to see bright colours and larger, more frequent images. The headings would potentially contain more puns and exclamation marks, and even the topics covered in the newspaper may be different.

Linking style, content and layout to the purpose

Each of the five main purposes of media products come with their own design requirements; style, content and layout of media products are adapted to get the purpose across. Table 1.6 shows these purposes and design requirements.

Table 1.6: The purpose and design requirements of media products

Purpose	Style, layout and content
Advertising/ promotional products	• Use persuasive language • Products or services look good or come across well • Use positive visuals and sound • Lead to an action
Educational products	• Usually contain both visuals and text • Make content accessible to the target audience • Have a formal structure • Contain detailed factual information
Entertainment products	• Hook the audience in through interesting, surprising, or even shocking use of images, text, video and/or audio • Evoke emotions in the target audience
Informational products	• Do not require emotional investment or enjoyment by the audience • Contain instructional information or facts • May not use many images or illustrations • Often have a serious or straightforward tone
Influential products	• Use persuasive language, images, video and text to convince an audience of the message • May use humour • May try to provoke a strong emotional reaction • Often contain a deep message or meaning

Over to you! 1

Find real-life examples of media products that are meeting each of these purposes.

- Advertise/promote
- Educate
- Entertain
- Inform
- Influence

What evidence is there in each product that demonstrates aspects of its purpose?

2.2 Client requirements and how they are defined

The client is generally the person or company who is financing the media product that is being created. This may include the owner of the company, and/or other staff who have been involved in the initial idea for the product. They will often have quite specific opinions on the style and content of the media product, though they can sometimes have very little idea as to how to achieve it and so come to a design team for all the answers.

Client briefs

A client brief is the key piece of information that any designer or creative team would need from the client to begin designing and planning a media product. The client brief will include several requirements that are necessary to make a successful product. It is the designer and the creative team's job to interpret these requirements to create a product that meets them.

Client brief formats

Client briefs come in all shapes and sizes. Some contain pages and pages of information, while others may just be a paragraph with some bullet points of ideas, or even less. On occasion, a client may already have an initial, or even a more detailed, idea that they would like to develop. This can be tricky if the initial idea does not work or cannot be turned into reality. Table 1.7 shows the different formats a client brief can take.

Table 1.7: Which brief format would you prefer to receive?

Client brief formats
Negotiated: The client and the design team would come together to discuss the needs of the client and the product they are asking for. An agreement is then reached for the design and creation process. An advantage of the negotiation process is that the design team have their opinions and ideas heard and the final idea combines the views of both parties. These briefs do often take longer to produce and can sometimes end up being quite different to what the client originally had in mind.
Meeting/discussion: The client talks about what they think they would like to achieve, and the design team takes notes. One difficulty with this approach is that details may be missed, or they may be written down wrongly or in a different way from what the client had initially said or intended.
Written: A recorded document that may be formal or informal and helps to guide the designers. This could be word processed or a presentation, but will provide enough detail that face-to-face meetings may not be necessary. This is particularly useful if the companies involved are very busy or work in different time zones.
Informal: An informal brief often means no official documentation, or the brief may lack detail. It could just be an idea or concept. There is often no set deadline either. There are many stories of clients who have scribbled their client brief for a designer on a napkin, or even given a brief verbally while in the lift on the way up to a meeting.
Formal: A clear and easy to understand written document that includes information about what the client wants to achieve and a timescale. It is not a contract or legal document, and the design team would usually gain further, detailed information through meetings with the client if needed.
Commission: A formal arrangement for a specific piece of work, usually between a larger company and a smaller one that they have chosen. There will be a clear contract and budget. For example, if a film was being made by Netflix, they may commission one or several much smaller, independent companies to create a font specifically for all of the film titles and credits. They will then use the one they feel is most appropriate. The larger company will have a lot of influence over the final product.

Client requirements

The purpose of a client brief is to provide information to the design and creative teams that will help them to produce a successful media product for the client that is also successful with the target audience. It will contain several different requirements that need to be met, and it is the designer's job to recognise and interpret the requirements correctly. These requirements will inform both the content and the types of documents used in the planning stage. Table 1.8 shows the potential client requirements found in a client brief.

Table 1.8: Potential client requirements found in a client brief

Client requirement	What it means
Purpose	The client will have a clear purpose for the product and a reason for it being created. The purpose will be one or more from advertising/promoting, educating, entertaining, informing and influencing.
Audience	This could be a very specific group of people, or a much larger one. Sometimes this will need refining and developing, but it will always heavily influence the style of the product.
Client ethos	This is the way the company wishes to be viewed, their reputation and the values they want to promote. These could be values of reliability, innovation, high quality or value for money.
Content	Content could be provided in a lot of detail or could be left up to the designer, but the basic elements of what the product will contain will be available.
Genre	Not all media products have a genre, but some briefs will have a very clear steer on the genre or type of product needed. This could be comedy, thriller, news, current affairs or family.
Style	Stylistic elements regarding colour, font and the look and feel of the product may be included. The client may say 'a futuristic feel' or 'a serious mood'.
Theme	A theme is a main subject or idea that everything hangs around. It may be based on a historical time period or season, or a concept such as love.
Timescale	This will state when the finished product is needed by. This may be negotiable, or it may be a fixed deadline.

Client briefs need to be read carefully, more than once, for all the requirements to be picked out as they may not always be clear. If there is a team working on the design, then it is likely that they will meet as a group to discuss the different requirements and to make sure that they all have the same understanding of the client brief.

Otherwise, this could lead to problems further into the project, at the planning stage (pre-production phase). Initial planning tools that could be used to interpret a client brief are a **mind map** (a diagram of ideas represented visually) and a **mood board** (an arrangement of images, materials, colours and fonts that convey a style or concept).

The requirements of clients can also be a **constraint** or restriction on both the planning and production stages – a specific choice of style or theme could make the planning much more difficult, and a tight timescale may mean that some of the designer's initial ideas cannot be completed at the production stage, so less complex or more simple ideas need to be used instead.

If a client wants to be represented in a certain way, based on their ethos or reputation, this can also be a constraint as it may stop the design team from coming up with other ideas that may have focused on other elements of the company. The same can be said for target audience. If a client has a specific target audience in mind, this immediately rules out any ideas that would not be suitable for that audience, even if they were brilliant and very creative.

Let's get creative!   1

Here is a client brief for a new comedy film that will be going straight out on Netflix, bypassing the cinemas.

"H-Team production company in association with Lakeside Pictures wishes to create a modern, family comedy called *Up and at 'em* based on a similar plot to the 1922 silent film of the same name. The feel of the movie is one of confusion and mischief, but never danger or threat. A cast of funny, colourful characters will be needed, and a new script due to the original film being silent.

This entertaining story is based around the robbery of some famous artworks and a hapless girl who borrows her father's car and manages to get herself involved in it. She then goes on to save the day and catch the criminals.

The movie will need to be set in the UK and must have both physical comedy and humorous lines in it. It would be good to add a Christmas theme to the narrative, as we want the film to come out ready for Christmas."

1   Are there any words you do not understand in this client brief? Research any words you are unsure of or any information you think you would need to know.

Continued

2   Create a mind map of all the requirements for this client. In brackets write which of the client requirement categories each one falls into.

3   What constraints can you find that have been created by these client requirements?

2.3 Audience demographics and segmentation

The words **demographic** and **segmentation** are used together a lot when discussing audience, so it is important to understand them and to know the difference between them.

> **Demographic + Segmentation = Target Audience**

Demographics are the different characteristics of the population, such as age, income, gender, race, ethnicity, marital status, education and employment. These different demographics can be broken down further to try to create the profile of people who are the target audience for a media product – this is called segmentation.

You could be targeting a new gaming podcast at 21–25 year old males, who have been in further education and are now in full-time employment; these are the demographics for the product. You could segment this audience further by adding in their needs, interests, geographical location or even opinions and behaviours.

So, this target audience could become much more specific – 21–25 year old males who are already into gaming and have enjoyed gaming since they completed their education. They now use gaming as a form of escapism from their full-time employment and wish to find out more about the games available to them and the stories behind how the games were made. They also have disposable income to buy the games that are recommended on the podcast.

Table 1.9 shows the categories that can be used for audience segmentation.

Table 1.9: What do you think would happen if audience demographics were not segmented any further?

Audience segmentation categories
Age: Age can be broken down into generations, school year or age groups, as well as in relation to family positions, e.g. Generation X; people who were born in the 1960s; 17–21 year olds; teenagers; grandparents.
Gender: An identity that relates to the socially constructed ideas of being male or female. People can identify as male, female, or can choose to be non-binary, e.g. females who view themselves as feminine; biological males that view themselves as women; females or males that view themselves as not being either female or male (non-binary).
Location: This relates to the specific place that the audience live or work. It could be a continent, country, region, county or even a specific town or city, e.g. people who live and work in the city of Liverpool.
Education: The level of learning that someone has. This could impact their understanding of or interest in a media product, e.g. some people stop education after achieving GCSEs, while others have a master's degree.
Income: The amount of money that a person either earns through their occupation or has coming into their account, e.g. managers earning £31 000 or more per year.
Interests and lifestyles: The pastimes, hobbies and activities that the audience is already interested in. Interests link closely with trends and can be part of someone's lifestyle – the way they choose to live their life, e.g. males who are into bodybuilding and have a very healthy lifestyle.
Ethnicity: People who belong to a social group that has common characteristics, cultural or national traditions, customs and beliefs that distinguish them from other groups, e.g. British Asian, White Scottish, Irish traveller, Black African, Muslim.
Occupation: A person's occupation is the job that they do. Different jobs require different levels of skill, knowledge and education, e.g. lawyers require a different level of education to cleaners.

The benefits of audience segmentation

Breaking down and identifying a target audience is an important stage for every media product, but what are the actual benefits of segmentation?

STICAMS (pronounced 'stickems') is a useful acronym for the benefits of audience segmentation. See Table 1.10 for the meaning of the STICAMS acronym.

Table 1.10: STICAMS (the benefits of audience segmentation)

Specific	Having a specific target audience means that you can focus your message on the right group of people who will be most likely to respond to your product.
Tailored message	Your message can be clear if it is aimed at a specific group of people, rather than being vague and general.
Identifiable	The target audience becomes a real group of people who can be used for focus groups and audience research.
Content matches preferences	Once you know who your audience is, you can ask them about their likes and dislikes to match the content of the product to their preferred ideas and opinions.
Achievable	Having a target audience group is much more likely to succeed than trying to include everyone. It also costs less and potentially takes less time.
Meeting needs	Once a target audience has been defined, research can be undertaken into what their needs or requirements are for the product.
Success that is measurable	A clear target audience is more easily measurable through gaining specific feedback from them. This can be matched against the client requirements.

Demographic influence

Audience demographics have a strong influence over the design and production of media products. Once a clear target audience has been identified, audience research can then take place to understand more about what they want, need and their spending/listening/viewing/reading behaviours. You may have a brilliant idea for a website, only to find out through audience research that they have no need for that style of website, or that they hate the idea! Then, it's back to the drawing board to come up with a different idea.

Case study

BBC iPlayer

BBC iPlayer, a web and mobile phone app for playing BBC TV programmes on demand, was launched in 2007. It was very successful and demonstrated the BBC's interest in using new technologies to provide content in creative ways.

The Guide to Researching Audiences Case Studies discussed how the BBC wanted to launch a new version of the iPlayer, called BBC iPlayer2, which would allow users to access both TV and radio programmes. In 2008,

Figure 1.13: iPlayer can be accessed on computers, tablets and mobile phones

the BBC commissioned research to gather existing users' reactions to the design of the new version.

The researchers segmented the audience based on accessibility and lifestyle into audience members who:

- watched TV only
- watched TV and listened to some radio
- mostly listened to the radio with some TV
- listened to the radio only.

They also placed importance on ensuring that radio users reflected all of the genres available (music, drama, comedy, news, documentary, etc.).

Because they segmented their audience in such detail, they were able to get additional feedback about the product's functionality for those who wanted to get to the radio features more quickly and easily. This meant that they could tweak their designs to allow users quicker access, along with the ability to listen to live radio.

In 2012, BBC iPlayer Radio was introduced and audio content removed from the original iPlayer app. In 2018 the BBC Sounds app was launched and now includes live radio, audio on demand and podcasts.

Without audience segmentation, the importance of the views of the radio users may never have been identified, resulting in a loss of users, rather than a product that has been continually developed to meet their needs.

Continued

Check your understanding

1   What was the reason for commissioning new audience research in 2008?

2   There are many ways that the researchers could have segmented their audience. What segmentation choices did they make?

3   Why do you think they segmented the audience in that way?

4   What other ways could the audiences have been segmented?

2.4 Research methods, sources and types of data

Conducting research is an important aspect of design, planning and production. It happens during all these stages and informs the detail of the product every step of the way, even once the product has seemingly been finished. Audience research can have a huge influence on the design of a media product.

An example of this is the film *Australia* (2008). It is an epic three-hour-long film directed by Baz Luhrmann, that initially had the main character, played by Hugh Jackman, dying at the end. Audiences at test screenings were not happy, so 20th Century Fox distributed a version to cinemas with a happy ending. Audiences have the power to change many aspects of a media product.

The media industry would not spend both time and money on audience research if it did not have its benefits. The idea behind audience research is that by asking questions about the media product being created, they will have more chance of success by the time the product has been finished. The designers and creators will have incorporated all useful feedback into the product so that it meets the needs of the target audience, and therefore sells more copies, influences the right people or gets the most viewers.

Primary and secondary research

If you are going to conduct audience research or competitor research, you would need to use a combination of **primary research methods** and **secondary research sources**. The data you generate from these research methods and sources needs to be valid and reliable.

- **Validity** is when the method you use to collect your data is measuring what you intended it to measure. For example, if you wanted to ask questions about favourite podcasts, but people responded about their favourite TV programmes, this data would not be valid.

- **Reliability** is how consistent and accurate the data is. For example, did you ask all your respondents the same questions? Did you change the way or the order in which you asked them? If you asked the questions again, would you get similar results?

It can be hard to make sure that research methods and sources are valid so that results are accurate and reliable.

Primary research methods

Primary research relates to first-hand accounts, data or opinions of something. The information will have come from someone who has had a direct connection with the product or idea so that they can give their views on it. Table 1.11 explains primary research and provides some examples.

Table 1.11: Primary research methods. Can you think of any others?

Primary research method	Explanation	Example
Focus groups	Groups of people who come together face-to-face or remotely to discuss an idea, product or campaign both before it has been created and before it has been distributed to the target audience. Their responses are recorded and analysed for useful comments and overall trends and opinions.	A group of parents of young children may be brought together to discuss a children's TV series aimed at toddlers.
Interviews	Meetings that are run on a one-to-one basis where in-depth questions can be asked to get detailed answers. This method is useful when specific contributions are needed.	To find out how easy a blind person finds accessing a new website to buy items.
Online surveys	These methods use online survey builders such as SurveyMonkey to create short-answer and multiple-choice questions that are quick and easy to analyse. The answers are collected and analysed instantly, providing minute-by-minute data and statistics.	A series of yes/no questions about the first episode of a new radio series.
Questionnaires	Often completed with a paper and pencil and can include a range of different question types, along with spaces to provide individual responses. These are often more difficult to analyse as they contain more detailed responses, in the person's own words.	A questionnaire about a person's emotional and physical response to a test screening of the latest John Lewis Christmas advert.

Secondary research sources

Secondary research is one step removed from the media product and is usually a second-hand account of relevant information. It sometimes quotes from or uses primary research, but it might also provide some analysis or commentary on the data that has been identified or collated. The person who wrote/recorded the secondary research was not actually involved in creating the product or idea. Table 1.12 gives some examples of secondary research types.

Table 1.12: When might you use each of these secondary research sources?

Secondary research source	Explanation	Example
Books and journals	Everything from textbooks to non-fiction books, articles in academic publications, called journals, and short papers on specific topics.	*Media, Culture and Society* is an academic journal and digital forum that can be accessed online.
Internet sites and research	This could involve browsing sites for background information, looking at social media sites for comments and feedback or viewing competitor products online.	Looking at the threads and comments on Facebook, Twitter and even TikTok after a TV programme has aired can give an idea of how well it has been received.
Magazines and newspapers	Most newspapers and magazines can be accessed online, but it is also possible to get old copies to look through to find specific articles or to look at audience reactions to new products and trends.	Magazine research is often a good place to start when researching genres and styles.
TV	Interviews, documentaries, news and review programmes are all useful to watch when researching into a specific area.	Even programmes like *Gogglebox* can give a real insight into audience opinion.

There are advantages and disadvantages to completing both primary and secondary research, and often it is necessary to complete both to gain a whole picture as they can provide different types of information.

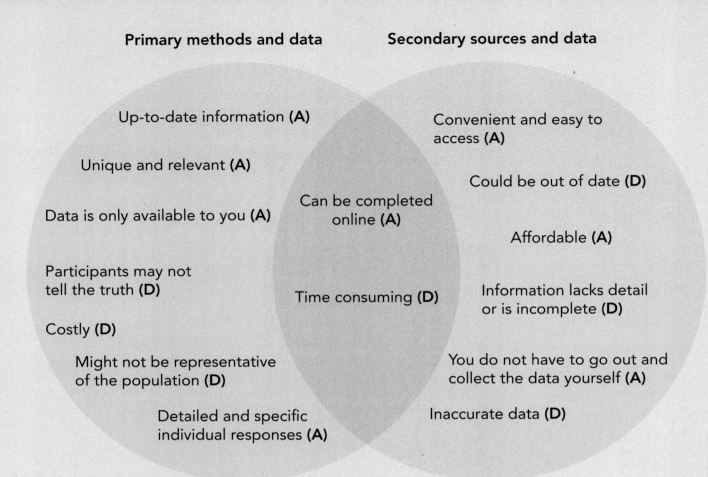

Primary methods and data

Secondary sources and data

Up-to-date information **(A)**

Unique and relevant **(A)**

Data is only available to you **(A)**

Participants may not tell the truth **(D)**

Costly **(D)**

Might not be representative of the population **(D)**

Detailed and specific individual responses **(A)**

Can be completed online **(A)**

Time consuming **(D)**

Convenient and easy to access **(A)**

Could be out of date **(D)**

Affordable **(A)**

Information lacks detail or is incomplete **(D)**

You do not have to go out and collect the data yourself **(A)**

Inaccurate data **(D)**

Figure 1.14: Media product research often utilises both types of research, considering both their advantages **(A)** and disadvantages **(D)**. Why do you think that is?

Research data

Both primary and secondary research provide us with two different types of data: qualitative and quantitative.

Qualitative data

Qualitative data (think quality, as in depth and detail) is data that is not based on numbers. This is not data that can be obtained from yes/no answers or multiple-choice questions. This is the detailed and individual information received through primary and secondary research such as content from focus groups, interviews and the longer response questions on questionnaires.

- **Advantages** of qualitative data are that it can often produce key relevant details that would not otherwise have been found out, along with useful quotes.

- **Disadvantages** of qualitative data are that it can be difficult and time consuming to analyse because it is hard to compare one response to another, but similar responses can still often be grouped together.

Quantitative data

Quantitative data (think quantity, as in lots of numbers) focuses on getting many responses and building up a picture through the analysis of the numbers generated. This data type is often called statistics.

- **Advantages** of quantitative data are that it gives a wider picture from more people, and that it is quicker and easier to analyse than qualitative data. Because of the limited options given for responses, they are often clearer and easier to analyse.

- **Disadvantages** are that quantitative data lacks the depth and detail of qualitative data, so you may not get the whole picture, or know the reasons why the statistics have come out the way they have.

Over to you!   2

Using an online survey builder, such as SurveyMonkey, create a five-question survey about a specific group of people's favourite films and genres.

- Think about how you might segment your audience to get specific and useful quantitative data.

- Create clear questions that have a limited number of options.

- Get 20 responses from your chosen target audience.

- Analyse the data to see what the results were.

1   What did you find out about the group of people?

2   Do you think this is representative of all members of this group?

3   What could you do to make the results more accurate or more reliable?

2.5 Media codes used to convey meaning, create impact and/or engage audiences

A **media code** is an element that is used to create or suggest meaning. The elements include sound, lighting, colour, text and graphics. For example, the lighting in a game show might be busy and bright, with bright white lights moving around a lot, but also use spotlights and darkness to focus in on contestants at key serious moments.

Media codes

There are three types of media code: technical codes, symbolic codes and written codes.

Technical codes

These are the ways in which different pieces of equipment are used to help tell a story, create a meaning or feeling, or have impact on an audience in that specific media form. The camera work in a film and the editing of those camera shots would be technical codes.

Symbolic codes

These codes are based on our understanding of society, culture and real life. They relate to the associated meanings we give objects, locations and actions. For instance, a character in an animated film may receive a beautiful bunch of flowers – the audience may assume that they are from someone who has a romantic relationship with that character, or that they are to say thank you, or even sorry, as this is often the case in real life.

Written codes

Written codes are the formal written language – words and phrases that are used in media products. The term 'written codes' actually relates not only to printed and written language on media products, but also language used in the media product. That is, spoken language such as dialogue, narration and song lyrics.

How meaning, impact and engagement are created

Media codes are used in many different media forms.

Animations

Animations are often used to improve or enhance a message or meaning for the audience, or to show something that would otherwise be too difficult to portray. These could be hand drawn, designed on the computer or developed using green screen technology.

In the most recent *Star Wars* films, some of the characters have been added in using Computer Generated Imagery (CGI). This is easier and quicker than designing and making puppets and prosthetics (fake body parts), which was done for the original *Star Wars* films of the 1970s and 1980s. There have even been instances of main characters being completely computer generated for some scenes. Figure 1.15 shows one of the sets of the *Star Wars* movies before the CGI characters have been added in.

Figure 1.15: Why do you think the makers of *Star Wars* chose a real location to film in rather than a studio?

Audio

Audio describes sound when it is recorded or broadcast. Sounds are very important in audio-only products such as podcasts and radio programmes, but they can be equally important in products using both audio and visual such as videos and TV programmes.

Audio can add a layer of depth to a scene in a film or create atmosphere on a podcast. The sounds could be recorded live using voices or props, created on a computer and added later, or produced by musical instruments and recorded as a soundtrack.

As an audience, we do not even notice most of the sounds that are happening in a media product on a conscious level, but our ears are taking it all in and our brains are processing what they hear to add further background information or emotion to what we are seeing or listening to. This creates an extra layer of subconscious meaning that will impact us, as the audience, drawing us in and engaging us with the product on a deeper level. Table 1.13 shows the impact and meaning of various audio types.

Table 1.13: Types of audio. Can you think of a product that uses more than one type of audio?

Audio type	Meaning and impact
Dialogue: Lines spoken by a character or voice-over	Dialogue is an effective tool to tell the audience key information or to move a narrative along to keep them engaged. When hearing dialogue we can tell how many people are interacting, where they are from and, often, their relationship to each other. This draws the audience in as they want to listen further to find out more.
Music genre: A type or style of music	The genre of music used in a media product can have a strong effect on the audience and can deepen their engagement with it. For example, using soft classical music, particularly with violins, can evoke sadness, while a rock 'n' roll song may indicate a fun party or gathering. We often connect the messages or emotions from music or songs that we know with the TV or radio programmes that they are used in.
Silence: The absence of sound	Silence happens surprisingly little in audio and audio-visual products; there is usually music or background noise. When used well, the complete absence of sound can indicate something very important, worrying or even scary. A scene in a horror film before the victim is revealed could have a second of silence, and the audience may also have stopped breathing, waiting to see what happens next. This adds to their sense of anxiety and fear and tells them that something big is about to happen, which keeps them engaged.
Sound effects: A sound other than speech or music	Usually these are added in post-production, but sound effect design needs to happen early on so that it is clear where extra impact will be added. Sound effects can be used to surprise, add impact or to add atmosphere and meaning to the on-screen dialogue or action. Sound effects can be used so that a person sounds like they are in the rain, when actually they are safe inside the recording studio.
Vocal intonation: The way in which dialogue is spoken	This is key to the feel of the media product, and the message that the audience will receive. Too loud and aggressive and the audience may feel they are being told off and disengage; too welcoming and friendly and they may not take the information seriously and may miss the meaning entirely. If a TV advert slogan voice-over sounds like it has a question at the end, it could leave audiences guessing whether or not the product really is as good as it says, meaning that it has no impact on their decision to buy the product.

Camera techniques

The three specific camera techniques of angles, shots and movement can happen individually or together. These techniques put the audience in a specific place in relation to the scenes unfolding in front of them and allow them to see only what the director wants them to see, so that the meaning is made clearer.

Camera angles

Camera angles are the angle at which the camera is pointed so that it captures the subject of the shot in a certain way. This choice of angle will give the audience messages about the characters, location and actions in the shot. A scene may be shot from several different angles; cutting between these different angles can evoke different experiences and emotions in a scene. Table 1.14 describes the various camera angles.

Table 1.14: Different camera angles

Camera angle	Description
Low angle	The camera is lower than the subject and is tilted upwards. This gives the impression of the subject having power or control. The audience is made to feel insignificant or powerless.
High angle	The camera is higher than the subject and is tilted downwards. This can be a matter of centimetres or can even be in the corner of the room as if it was a CCTV camera. This can create a feeling of surveillance or observation. It can also make the subject appear powerless or unaware of something, and the audience point of view may feel more superior.
Eye level	The camera is placed at the same level as the character's eyes in the shot. This is sometimes called an eyeline match, if it is used with more than one character in a scene. This is the most natural camera level and simulates what a human might see in real life. When an eye level angle is contrasted with other angles in a scene, those angles have much more of an impact.
Dutch angle, canted angle or tilt shot	The camera needs to be on a slightly sideways angle, so that the viewpoint is similar to someone tilting their head slightly to the side. This angle can be used to make the audience feel uneasy or out of control. It can also signal that something is wrong or unsettling or that the character is disorientated.
Bird's eye/ aerial view or overhead shot	Often taken using a drone, crane or a helicopter, this angle is taken from very high up, often looking down at a 90-degree angle. This can make the actors or objects below seem very small and short, showing that they are just a tiny part of a much wider story or location. They can also be used effectively to film chase scenes.
Worm's eye view	This angle requires the camera to be on the floor, as if it was a worm, looking up at an object from far below. This can be used to make a person or object look tall, strong and mighty. It may make the audience feel powerless or lost.

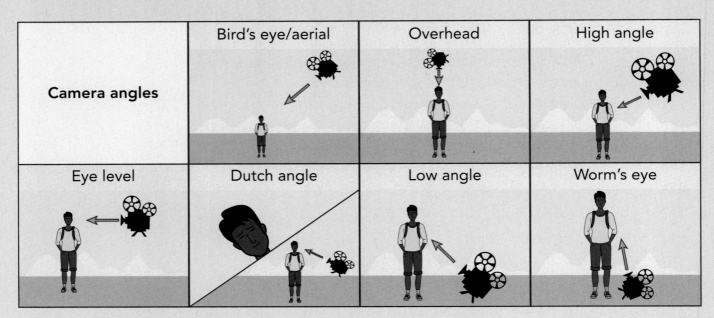

Figure 1.16: This is what each camera angle might look like. Can you try these using a phone or tablet?

Camera shots

A camera shot is the way the camera has been set up to start rolling, to film a scene. Footage is created from whatever position the camera has been placed in, and these shots are placed one after the other to build up a scene. Camera shots are all about composition and placement of the subject or objects in the frame to tell a story. Table 1.15 describes the various camera shots.

Table 1.15: Different camera shots. Try them out to see if you can set up the perfect shot

Camera shot	Description
Long shot/wide shot	Shows the whole of an object or person, in relation to their surroundings and location. It allows the audience to see characters in an environment and can reveal more information about them. In an extreme long shot, the person or object will not be much more than a tiny ant-sized image. The impact on the audience is that they feel the person or object is insignificant, or that they have a huge task ahead of them.
Establishing shot	A shot with a clear location or building framed within it that informs the audience where the scenes after it are going to take place, adding meaning to the location. This could be a shot of a creepy old house, a school, or even a car.
Medium or mid shot	Medium shots tend to show an actor from the waist up; it means that the audience can see both the body language and facial expressions of the person, as well as getting further information about the surroundings they are in – both of which will engage them by making them want to know more. A mid shot can also be used to show a character from the waist down. For example, if a person was running, a mid shot may be of their legs and shoes. The impact of this could be that the audience wonders where they are running to or why they are running.

Table 1.15: Continued

Camera shot	Description
Close up/extreme close up	This shot will be very close to the subject, so that only their head or face is shown. The audience can see facial expressions in detail but can't see the location, or what may be provoking those expressions. This tends to be for added emotional effect. The impact on the audience is that they may feel closer to the character and begin to care about them. Objects can also be filmed in close up, which suggests that they may be significant to the storyline.
Two shot	A mid shot that focuses on two people who are next to each other, or one in the foreground and one in the background. This engages the audience who want to understand the relationship between the two people.
Over the shoulder shot	The camera is placed behind the character, on the left- or right-hand side, so that it sits just behind the shoulder. This helps the audience to understand what the character is seeing, making the meaning clearer to them.
Point of view shot	The camera is set up in place of where the character's head would usually be and shows what they can see directly from their point of view. This can engage the audience as it puts them in the position of a character in a physical way, so that they feel the emotions of that character.

Figure 1.17: Can you think of examples you have seen on TV or in a film of these camera shots?

Camera movement

Cameras will stay still for a lot of the shots and angles that have been discussed, but on occasion adding in some camera movements will help to emphasise a particular point that needs engaging with by the audience. Table 1.16 describes the various camera movements.

Table 1.16: Different camera movements. Can you spot any of these movements in films you have seen?

Camera movements	Description
Tilt	The camera stays in one place but is tilted up or down in a similar way to what a person would do if they were to look slowly down at their shoes or up to the top of a building. If a camera tilts upwards to show how tall something is, this may create an impression of the character feeling weak or powerless.
Track	A camera is mounted on a little cart with wheels, called a dolly, which is then set up on a track. The camera can then move along the track sideways, forwards and backwards in order to move along with the action. This gives the audience the feeling of being involved in the action, for example in a horse race they may feel like they are going along on the ride with them.
Pan	The camera stays in one place, but swivels from left to right or right to left to follow the action as it goes past or to 'look' from one side of the room to the other. The impact of this can be the feeling of speed, or it can copy the feeling of turning your head to look at something more closely.
Zoom	The camera will stay still but zoom in or out so that the subject becomes bigger or smaller and more or less of the surroundings can be seen. Zooming in to get people's reactions on a live tennis final, for example, may add to the tension and emotion of the situation.

Figure 1.18: What effect does a lot of movement have on the feel or tone of a media product?

Let's get creative! 2

1 Find a trailer for a film of your choice and select a 15-second section of it.

2 Watch the section a few times to get an idea of what shots, angles and movements are in it.

3 Using the pause button, go through shot-by-shot and log each shot, angle and movement that is used.

4 Create a storyboard that accurately portrays the action you see and looks like the shots, angles and movements used.

Colour

Colour plays an important role in engaging an audience – choose the wrong colour scheme and your media product could have little impact and will fade into the background, or even worse will actually make people choose another product as they dislike it so much. Colours are used in all elements of visual design, from magazines and comics to websites and apps.

Colour is also used in film and TV programmes to create a mood or feeling, or to attract attention to specific objects so that the audience engages with them. Colours have meanings associated with them, just like objects do.

For example, if a British or Irish web user was to see an image of a black cat on a website selling sunglasses, it may remind them of good luck so they may find it appealing. In many other areas of Europe, the use of a black cat may signify bad luck.

These associated meanings are also called **connotations** (see Unit R094, Topic Area 1, 'Colour palette and meaning').

Figure 1.19: How does this cat with sunglasses make you feel?

Graphics

Graphics are visual images, that have been created either by hand or on the computer, which represent or enhance the message that the product is trying to convey. They can be created in both two-dimensional (2D) and three-dimensional (3D) forms and will change in style dependent on the purpose of the graphic and the context that it is to be used in.

Graphics could be:

- diagrams
- illustrations
- drawings
- cartoon characters

- logos
- abstract shapes
- patterns

Text or sound is often used to anchor the meaning of the graphic, to add clarity to it. The creation and placement of these graphics to fit a particular purpose is called **graphic design**. Computer software such as Adobe Photoshop is used by graphic designers to create a final product, or an aspect of a larger product.

Interactivity

Many media products are interactive, meaning that the audience can take control of them in some way. Audiences can choose their responses to the media product in front of them, and the action that they take will result in a new and different element being made available to them. One of the clearest examples of an interactive product is a computer game – a player makes choices second-by-second and the game responds to each of those choices by changing the outcome.

More recently, digital magazines, newspapers and even books have become more interactive, as we can click on embedded links, highlight text and even make notes on the products we are reading.

Websites, kiosks and apps that are intended to inform their audience are excellent examples of interactivity – the user can click on a video or gallery, a drop down menu or a form. Once they have clicked, the next choice is then made available to them.

Figure 1.20: An interactive product on a car graphical display. Where else are such interactive products used?

Adverts and TV programmes are developing more interactivity. For example, you can choose which advert you would like to watch during an ad break, or even decide what the adventurer Bear Grylls does next in his programme *You vs. Wild*. The purpose of these interactive features is to both inform and entertain, so that they are more memorable.

Lighting

Lighting refers to the use of natural light, indoor light sources and specialist lighting to light the objects within a shot for maximum impact. It is obvious that if products were not lit properly then we would not be able to see them, but lighting is about much more than just the function of seeing objects. The way a scene, person or product is lit gives us subconscious messages that help the audience to make meaning of what they are seeing. Depending on the purpose of the product, lighting can add drama, create depth and enhance images to add impact to a scene. Table 1.17 shows the functions of lighting.

Table 1.17: Functions of lighting. Can you find any other examples?

Function of lighting	Example
Tells the audience what they should be looking at. It guides them to where a specific prop, actor or reaction is coming from.	If the action outside a window is well lit, and the rest of the room is in darkness, our eye would be drawn to what we can see out of the window.
Tells the audience about the characters. It can pick up on specific facial expressions or reactions, and the use of shadows can give us clues to the thoughts or personality of the character.	Shadows across the face could mean that the character is not to be trusted or has something to hide.
Reflects the genre of film, TV programme, photograph, video game or advert.	Comedy, news and upbeat advertising will usually require bright lighting. A horror film or advertising for a very sophisticated product may require low lighting to create shadows and darkness.

Intensity and levels

The words intensity and levels both refer to a light's brightness, and the output of light. If the lighting intensity is too low, a camera can struggle to pick out individual features of objects in the frame. If lighting levels are too high, details will again be lost but this time because everything is too bright, as too much light is passing through the camera lens. When details are lost, the audience engagement will be low because they will struggle to know what they should be looking at.

Individual lights can be dimmed or brightened with switches and bulbs, the size of the lights can be controlled, and light can be blocked out or

Figure 1.21: What is the effect of bright, intense lighting in this image?

even diffused. For example, if a thin material is placed over a window it can spread or diffuse the light more evenly to reduce glare coming from one place.

The primary source of light used when filming is called the **key light** and it is usually the brightest one. The key light will be focused on and pointing towards the subject of the frame, but it can be placed anywhere. The key light is often supported by secondary lights that are not quite as bright, called **fill lights**, which will help to balance out the light in the scene to create a more natural look or to create shadows. If the purpose of a media product such as a news bulletin is to inform, then the audience would expect to see bright, high key lighting with few shadows. This would convey a message of honesty, calm and transparency, showing the news programme has nothing to hide.

Figure 1.22: How many lights are there, and which are the fill lights?

Positioning

Positioning relates to the way that lights are placed in a scene, both in terms of location and angle. When lights are positioned in specific ways, a new meaning is created or enhanced for the audience to subconsciously spot. Table 1.18 shows the different lighting positions and their effect on the audience.

Table 1.18: Lighting positions. What camera shots could be combined with these?

Lighting position	Description	Effect on the audience
Front lighting	The light is directly in front of the subject.	Can be flat and make the subject look shocked. It may tell the audience that the subject is being interviewed or interrogated.
Three quarter lighting	The light is placed at a 45-degree angle to the subject.	This is the most popular place for a high key light because it gives the subject depth so that the audience feel connected to a real person.
Back lighting	The light is placed behind the subject, out of shot.	Can create a silhouette, throwing the subject in shadow. This could engage the audience as they want to see the character revealed.

Table 1.18: Continued

Lighting position	Description	Effect on the audience
Side lighting	The light is placed directly to the side of the subject.	Can show one side of a subject in light and the other in darkness. Audiences may feel the character is moody, has something to hide, or has two sides to their personality.
Practical lighting	The lights in the scene: lamps, candles, ceiling lights or fire	Used to create atmosphere and to make locations seem more real and natural. Use of candles can mean romance, magic or luxury.
Low angle lighting	A light placed directly below the subject	Used to make the character appear scary or dangerous. Often used to signify the arrival of the villain.

Mise-en-scène

The phrase mise-en-scène can be roughly translated from French to mean 'everything in the right place in the frame'. This term relates to how props, costumes, hair, make-up, scenery and actors are placed in a shot or scene. Controlling these elements so that they all fit together well can create a powerful and memorable image to look at that will have a strong impact on the audience and keep them engaged. Table 1.19 outlines the elements of mise-en-scène and gives explanations.

Table 1.19: Elements of mise-en-scène. Can you apply these to a scene from a TV programme or video game you know of?

Mise-en-scène element	Explanation
Props	Any objects that are in the frame. These could be objects that the actor interacts with, or ones that have been placed around the set or location. Some props have a clear meaning within the storyline; some of them are there to make the set or location more believable and engaging.
Costumes, hair and make-up	All the clothing worn in any scene is referred to as a 'costume'. It needs to fit the actor, and suit the character and the location, period and genre. 'Hair' could relate to styling of an actor's own hair or the fitting of wigs, extensions or bald caps. 'Make-up' refers to anything put on the actor's face, hands or body to create the character. This could include wounds, prosthetics, tattoos, body paint and theatrical make-up. Hair and make-up can take hours to apply, but the impact on the audience is in the believability of the characters.
Scenery	Location and the setting are important to engage the audience by introducing them to the surroundings in which action will happen. Scenery engages audiences as it allows them to understand more about where a character lives or works and how he or she fits in with the environment.
Actors	What the actors look like, how they interact with others and where they stand, sit or lie in a scene are key elements of mise-en-scène. An actor can easily look awkward or like he or she does not belong if their actions, body language and posture are not fitting with the other elements in the scene.

Figure 1.23 shows all the elements of mise-en-scène working together for the purpose of entertaining an audience.

Scenery:

Castle location. Scene is set in front of the castle to show the characters defending it. This adds to the impact of the action in the scene.

Actors:

Stood together signifying a relationship between them. Soldier's hands on swords suggest defensive behaviour along with his frowning, alert expression. The Queen has a defensive posture too, gripping her cloak around her, but raising her face to the threat, she also looks defiant and strong.

Costume:

Crown with jewels signifying royalty, nobility and power. The soldier does not have one, so we can assume he is not the king, but is one of the noble woman's subjects, defending her.

Costume:

Armour and cape suggesting battle and war/adventure genre.

Prop:

Authentic looking sword adds meaning to the character and scene.

Costume:

Chain mail to signify he is a soldier as well as the period the film is set in.

Hair and make-up:

Intricate plaits are reminiscent of Viking braids and can be a symbol of strength and wisdom. When compared with the soldier's rugged haircut and beard, they suggest the character is not a soldier.

Scenery:

Artificial snow used to create seasonal, cold feeling.

Costume:

Robe of purple and orange. Suggests royalty, wealth, strength and the wisdom of a leader.

Costume:

Large silver ring with red jewel. Suggests wealth, power, action and passion.

Prop:

Second sword, showing the character is a warrior as well as the genre of the film.

Figure 1.23: How important do you think mise-en-scène is to creating genre-based media products?

Movement

The term movement relates to characters and objects moving within a frame. When characters or objects move, the audience's eyes are drawn to them, providing an opportunity for engagement in a visual way. The movement between characters or objects is a source of energy for the media product and can add more to a story, over and above the dialogue. Movement of a logo in the top corner of a website can make it more memorable, in the same way as seeing a product in an advert being used or moved will bring it to life.

The more that objects or actors are moving, and the speed at which they move, will produce action and energy, creating an impact on the audience even if the camera itself is still. There may be more, or less, movement within a frame dependent on genre, purpose and the type of media product being created.

Stretch

Watch the trailer for Netflix's interactive programme *Carmen Sandiego: To Steal or Not to Steal*. This programme combines animation, interactivity and the spy/thriller/crime genre to create a programme where the audience get to choose how it progresses. It has been very successful.

1   Analyse how media elements have been combined. Look back through the current section 'How meaning, impact and engagement are created' to remind yourself of the media elements to consider.

2   Explain why you think *Carmen Sandiego* has been such a success.

Transitions move the eye from one shot or slide to the next. These are applied during editing in post-production. The most common transition from one shot to the next is a cut, but lots of other transitions can be used to create different meanings and add a tone or mood to a film scene, app, game or other interactive media product.

- **Cut:** One piece of footage is put directly next to another, with one shot ending where the next one begins. This could be two shots of the same scene, or the second shot could move the action to a new scene, location and time. It creates a basic link between shots to build a narrative for an audience.

- **Dissolve:** One clip will literally seem to fade or dissolve away, revealing another clip underneath it. This is achieved by the first clip becoming lighter and more transparent, with the clip underneath fading in and eventually taking the place of the first clip. This happens in a subtle way so that audiences may not even spot it. A dissolve can be used to mean action and time moving on, or even create a sense of despair and longing for something or someone. This can be used when the purpose of the product is to advertise or entertain.

- **Cutaway:** A shot will 'cut away' to another shot that could be in the same scene but could also be in a different location or time. There will then be a cut back to the original scene and shot where the action will carry on. This can be used for flashbacks, comedy reactions or to show the audience action that is occurring at the same time. Cutaway is used in the sitcom *Family Guy* to show Stewie's reaction to his embarrassing parents.

Figure 1.24: What do you think Stewie's reaction is in this cutaway?

- **Wipe:** This 'wipes' one shot from the frame, replacing it with one coming in from another direction. This is often used to show the passage of time, maybe a jump of a few hours or days. Wipe is used heavily in the *Star Wars* films and *The Mandalorian* TV programme.

- **Fade:** This is very common, and is mainly used at the start and end of a scene, or when a character dies in a video game to create a sense of finality. The image becomes lighter to fade out to white, or darker to fade to a black screen. Fading to black signifies closure for the audience, while a fade to white can be less obvious and leave the audience without a clear sense of an ending. It can work well in entertainment products and advertising.

- **Split cut/sound bridge:** The audio and video are split from each other, and transition to the next shot at different times. In a split cut, the video shot changes before the sound does. In a sound bridge, the sound of the next scene generally begins before the visuals. This creates a meaning or link between the two shots for the audience, engaging them further with the story by connecting the two shots together. In *The Lost World: Jurassic Park*, a shot of a woman screaming cuts to a shot of main character yawning, while the sound of the scream is still going. The sound then becomes the screeching of a subway car slowing down, linking them all together.

- **Match cut:** This is where the placing of the objects or people within the shot match up. It could be moving from a long shot to a close up where the actor is posed in the same way, or even shots of two different locations in which the same object is set up in the same place in both. An example could be several shots of different locations all with match cuts showing a red telephone box in the bottom right-hand corner. The impact on the audience is that they understand these telephone boxes are somehow linked and want to know how and why.

- **Jump cut:** A longer piece of filmed footage is broken into three sections, and the middle section is taken out, so that the action 'jumps' from one shot to another. The impact on the audience is the feeling of having jumped through time or location slightly. This is often used to create excitement or energy within a sequence. The *Nike: Make Every Yard Count* advert makes use of many jump cuts, one after the other, to show different people in different locations all playing cricket in a similar way.

Typography

Typography is an art form that involves creating a specific style and arrangement of letters to make the words clear, readable and appealing to look at. It is used in product design to create meaning and impact, and to engage consumers. To learn more about the elements of typography see Unit R094, Topic Area 2, 'Typography'.

How content, codes and conventions work together

Symbolic codes and technical codes work alongside each other to provide the building blocks of all media products. Combined with content that has been created with a clear purpose in mind, they can form a powerful product that can convey meaning to an audience that can have a huge impact on them.

Written codes will have an impact on the audience through what they read and what they hear. Their meaning is enhanced in a media product by the symbolic and technical codes used in combination with them.

The symbolic codes that the audience experience allow them to make cultural and real-life connections to the media product they are accessing.

The technical codes that are used will enhance those connections and develop the storyline to hook the audience in and keep them there so that the message can be conveyed effectively.

Review your learning

Test your knowledge

Using all of the symbolic, technical and written codes outlined above, analyse the following media products and answer the questions:

- the first minute of the opening sequence of a film of your choice
- a print advert for a product of your choice
- a website for a well-known attraction or event.

1   What is the purpose of each product and what technical, symbolic and written codes have been used?

2   What connotations or associated meanings were created?

3   How have the audience been engaged and/or impacted by these symbolic, technical and written codes?

What have you learnt?

	See section
• How style, content and layout are linked to the purpose.	2.1
• Client requirements and how they are defined.	2.2
• Audience demographics and segmentation.	2.3
• Research methods, sources and types of data.	2.4
• How media codes are used to convey meaning, create impact and/or engage audiences.	2.5

TA3

Pre-production planning

Let's get started

Why is planning so important in the media industry? What do you think would happen if media products were created without planning?

Figure 1.25: Concept art is just one example of planning. Can you think of others?

What will you learn?

- Work planning.
- Documents used to support ideas generation.
- Documents used to design and plan media products.
- The legal issues that affect media.

3.1 Work planning

You may think that making a media product cannot be that complicated, so it is worth trying to do without planning. After all, what could possibly go wrong? However, the purpose of planning is to make sure the technical and creative teams have a clear brief as to what they are creating and know their responsibilities. Without planning they would not know what could go wrong, so may encounter problems they had not expected. This may result in delays, extra costs and may even lead to the cancellation of the product entirely. Planning is so important to the success of a project that it's not worth the risk not to do it. Figure 1.26 shows six key reasons for work planning.

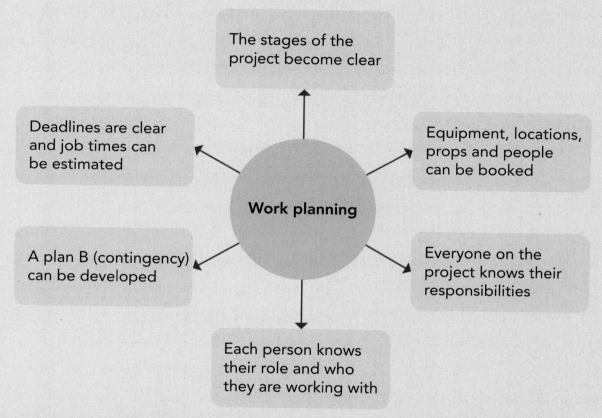

Figure 1.26: Key reasons for work planning. Do you plan your work out before completing it?

Workplans

A workplan is the document you use for work planning and to track **workflow**. It is a live, working document that can be edited and updated as the project moves along. Sometimes timescales shift or activities take longer than expected, so it needs to be a true reflection of the whole project that everyone on a project team can work from. A workplan will contain **milestones** that relate to the dates given by the client for completion of the product. Each project will be made up of at least three production phases. To learn more about the production phases of a project see Topic Area 1, 'Production phases'.

Activities:
Smaller actions to be carried out to complete a task.

Resources:
Hardware, people and software needed to run a project.

Timescales:
The length of time available to complete the project including all phases, or any of the specific tasks and activities within the project. The end of a project timescale is called a deadline.

Contingencies:
A set of events or problems that might occur during a project along with a brief plan for how to respond to each one.

Phases:
Pre-production, production and post-production stages of a project.

Tasks:
Larger pieces of work.

Workflow:
All the activities in the order they need to be completed. Some can be completed at the same time as others, while some can only be completed one after the other.

Milestones:
Key points in a project, e.g. the product has been created or the marketing campaign is launched. Milestones do not usually impact the length of the project but are markers to help check progress.

Figure 1.27: The role of workplan components. What do you think are the most important components?

How workplans are used

There are many uses for a workplan, all of them relating to project management. The main uses of workplans are outlined here.

- **To manage time effectively:** It could cover the months, weeks and days that the project will run for, as well as how many hours specific activities should take. This provides a useful guide for checking on the progress of the project. If some activities are taking longer than expected, then the workplan can be updated to reflect reality. It tells the project team whether they are ahead or behind where they should be.

- **For outlining tasks and activities clearly:** Everyone knows the task requirements, the activities that need to be completed to finish each task, and the order in which the activities need to be completed. This ensures that no-one jumps ahead or misses out an important activity.

- **To manage resources:** A list of resources for each task makes it clear what equipment will be needed during a project, so it can be booked in advance. It is a reminder of what to use/bring nearer the time and to check that resources work ahead of time. It also means that software can be downloaded/updated ready for the activities to be completed without causing a delay to the project.

Sharing a workplan between a team helps to keep everyone on track, and is important for planning work if you are working on a project by yourself. Workplans can help you stay focused and motivated, as well as breaking a big project down into manageable chunks. They can also remind you of the end goal and show you what you have achieved at every stage.

Advantages of using workplans

There are several advantages to using workplans to plan media products: some for those people directly using the workplans and some that apply to anyone involved in the project. Table 1.20 explains the advantages of using workplans.

Table 1.20: The advantages of using workplans

Advantage	Explanation
Allows a production manager or project manager to see all stages of a project	Sometimes it can be hard to oversee a whole project and know everything that is going on – a workplan helps to keep track of who, what and when.
Everyone knows their roles and responsibilities	Each team member can use the workplan to remind themselves what they should be doing and when.
People will know exactly when they will be needed	By planning in who is needed for each activity, people can add the dates to their own diaries so that they are ready to complete the task on time.
Progress and achievements can be tracked	A live (regularly updated) workplan enables achievements and progress to be celebrated, which will motivate the team.
There are clear goals and deadlines	If there are clear, shared goals and deadlines there is more chance of these being met by the team.
The running of the project can be evaluated against the workplan	The work completed can be compared with the rate at which it was supposed to be completed, so judgements about how the project has gone so far can be made, and specific areas then improved.
Ensures resources and budget are used accurately	Appropriate people for the project will be lined up, along with the right equipment in the right quantities. So, the budget will not be wasted.
Allows the users to plan for the possibility of things going wrong	By using **contingencies** on the workplan, possible scenarios can be thought through that might possibly cause a problem, along with ways to solve those problems.
It is quick and easy to establish if something is going wrong	Having a document with clear deadlines, tasks and activities means that if something is completed in the wrong way or there is likely to be a delay, it can be spotted quickly before it impacts the rest of the project.

Over to you!   **1**

Choose any project that you have coming up. It could be a homework project, a product you have been asked to create or an activity you must complete as a group.

1 Using either a spreadsheet, word-processing document, or pen and paper, create a workplan with columns and rows. The first four column headings should be:

- Tasks
- Activities
- Timescales
- Resources.

2 Can you think of anything that might go wrong during the project? How could you solve these problems? Add and fill in a 'Contingencies' column.

3 Identify who you think might need a copy of your workplan.

3.2 Documents used to support ideas generation

The first stage of the pre-production phase is to understand and interpret the client requirements from the client brief. Once you have done this, design ideas will need to be generated. There are two main documents which are very helpful with this task – a mind map and a mood board.

Mind maps and mood boards are covered in Unit R094, Topic Area 2, 'Pre-production documents for planning visual identity and digital graphics'.

3.3 Documents used to design and plan media products

There are several useful documents that will help you to design and plan media products. They each have their own purposes and they will not all be useful in every situation: sometimes one document will be much more suitable than others and sometimes a few different documents are needed.

Asset log

The purpose of an asset log is to organise and categorise any **assets** that have been collected to use in a media product. It is a digital spreadsheet, database or table which is continually updated throughout a project. The term assets may relate to illustrations, photos, diagrams, fonts, videos or sounds.

The asset log will include a list of the assets, with a link or description of each one that ideally can be sorted, searched and filtered. The log is then stored somewhere that is easily accessible by all creative and technical team members so that they can contribute to the log when needed or use it to find a particular asset. The asset log also provides an opportunity to include **copyright** information and who the copyright holder is.

An asset log is effective because all members of the team can access the latest, most up-to-date version of the document at any time and they all have the same information. This means that everyone is using the same set of assets, which helps with branding and consistency of style. Asset logs are appropriate for all media products and can be used at any time in the planning and production stages.

You can improve the effectiveness of an asset log by ensuring it only contains relevant information. If an asset log contains too much information that is not relevant, it can become too large to contribute to effectively and it can be difficult to find the useful assets amongst the less useful ones.

Flow chart

A flow chart is a diagram of events or steps that show the order they should happen in. It is appropriate to use whenever there is a process or project that needs to be broken down into steps. Its purpose is to show how the work **flows** from one task to the next in a logical way, from start to finish, and provides instructions about how to complete specific tasks. It can also show which people and tasks come before and after any specific step in the project.

Flow charts are usually digital documents created in word-processing software or a specific flow chart app. Flow charts use shapes containing information connected using lines and directional arrows. An oval or circle will usually represent the start and end points of the process, while rectangles are used to show the steps between those points. There are often decisions to be made, which result in rectangles with yes/no responses in them. Depending on which answer is chosen, there will be a different flow chart path to follow with new instructions. Figure 1.28 is an example of a flow chart, outlining the process for sourcing, editing, saving and logging assets.

A flow chart can be very effective in getting complex processes across in a visual way. You can break a whole project down into its component parts so that all creative, technical and senior team members know what they are doing.

To improve the effectiveness of a flow chart you would need to outline a project or process with a specific start and finish point. If the project is too big to represent in a flow chart there may be too many steps, making it seem too complicated. If the steps are too vague, then what needs to be done will not come across in a clear way.

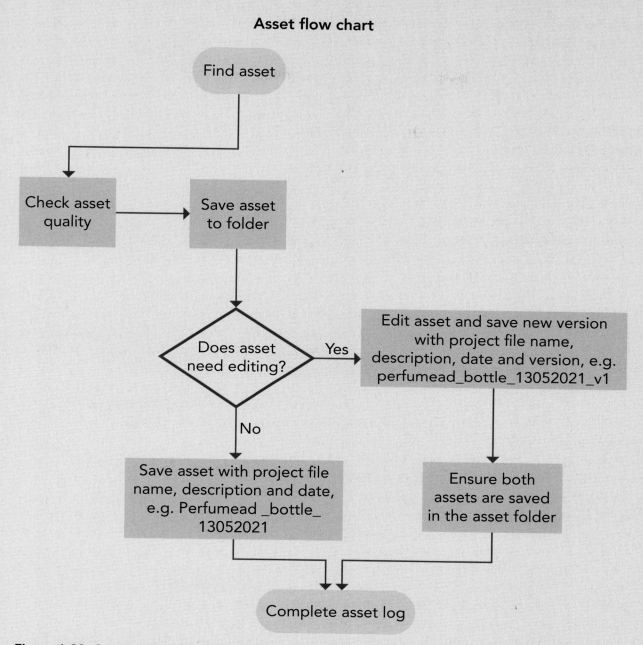

Asset flow chart

Figure 1.28: Can you think of some uses you may have for a flow chart in your school or home life?

Script

A script is a document that contains the written text of a media product laid out in a very specific way. Sometimes these documents are first handwritten, but because there are usually several versions of a script before the final one is used, it tends to be completed on word-processing software to allow for easy editing. There are also script templates and formatting apps available.

It includes the dialogue that people say, their movements, actions, expressions and instructions on how the lines should be said. Scripts are used for audio and audio-visual products, and are appropriate for visual storytelling such as comics and graphic novels too. A script will also contain music cues, sound effects and information about the scenes, which will run in **chronological order** in the final product, therefore it is useful for everyone involved in a production whether in creative, technical or senior roles.

Scripts are effective because they break down the story into a functional process. They provide the necessary elements to create a full scene in a clear and well-organised way. If you use character names next to the dialogue in a script, you can easily see what each character has to say and when.

Figure 1.29, on the next page, shows a script for part of a scene for a luxury car TV advert.

A script cannot show any of the elements in a visual way, so although a location may be described as an exterior location, we cannot see what it will look like in the document. A script's effectiveness can be improved by turning it into a **shooting script** containing the camera shots and angles.

Storyboard

A storyboard is a series of boxes or panels containing the action that occurs, shot-by-shot, in an audio-visual product. The boxes show what each shot will look like from a specific camera angle and shot type. Underneath, you would usually include some directions and instructions relating to camera shot, angle and movement. There might also be a description of the action in the scene, sound cues and even transitions required to connect one shot to the next.

It is most appropriate for visually representing the storyline of a live action or animation film, TV programme, game or advert to show the sequence that the action needs to happen in. Storyboards are highly effective for camera operators, lighting and sound engineers, the director, actors and even the costume, hair and make-up teams so that they all know what each scene requires.

Detailed and precise storyboards can make filming quick and easy to complete, but they can be just as effective as a starting point for a creative and technical team to use as a framework for their ideas once they are on set. Detailed storyboards are likely to be created digitally but more simple ones may be hand drawn.

EXT. WINDING ROAD THROUGH MOUNTAINS IN A SUNNY LOCATION – DAY

A brand new soft top sports car smoothly winds its way along the road around the mountain, approaching a CAFÉ at the very top of the mountain. A woman, SUZANNA is driving, there is no one else in the car. Modern music plays from the car radio. She wears a SUMMER DRESS, SUNGLASSES and DRIVING GLOVES. She pulls up to the café, we hear the tyres on the gravel. She turns off the engine. She looks towards the café and smiles.

SUZANNA

Mama, Mama, I'm back!

An older woman comes to the café door and looks out. She puts her hand to her mouth.

MAMA

(Gasps) Suzanna, is that you? I can't believe it!

SUZANNA

(Shyly) I told you I would come back.

Suzanna smiles and gets out of the car. She leaves the door open and walks to Mama, who begins to protest.

MAMA

But you can't leave the car like that, all open, what if it rains? What if someone steals it?

Suzanna smiles again, looks back at the car, turns away from it again and presses a button on her watch. The door closes and the roof comes up out of the back of the car. Mama laughs and claps her hands together then leads the way inside. We see the car headlights dim as if it is going to sleep.

VOICE OVER

(smooth and warm) This is a car that does almost everything for you.

A car you can communicate with from inside your house, or wherever you are.

Figure 1.29: Can you picture what this script might look like when filmed?

There are limitations to how effective a storyboard can be, as you cannot include all the information required for shooting or creating footage. It cannot, for example, show all the dialogue in a scene, or detail of what props and costumes are required.

You can improve the effectiveness of storyboards by clearly outlining the key information for different users. For example, the make-up artist may only wish to see the information relevant to them.

Figure 1.30: Tom Cruise and director Brian De Palma on the set of the film *Mission: Impossible*, 1996. Did you know that storyboards are taken on set as visual reminders?

Visualisation diagram

A visualisation diagram is a detailed drawing or sketch that shows what a final media product should look like. To learn about visualisation diagrams, see Unit R094, Topic Area 2, 'Visualisation diagrams'.

Wireframe layout

A wireframe layout is a digital or hand drawn line drawing that shows the layout for and arrangement of assets for a page or slide of a media product. If a product has more than one page, like a website, then you could draw a wireframe layout for each page, which will make the similarities and differences between pages clear.

The purpose of a wireframe layout diagram is to show the layout of an interactive media product and outline functionality for the designer. As the focus is on layout and function rather than appearance you can use rectangles and other shapes to show where different elements such as images, videos and buttons will go. You might also want to include a brief mention of what the content is and/or the interactivity that will take place to check that these are all usable.

What wireframe layouts do not do is show elements of **house style**. This makes them appropriate for creating master slides and page structures, as it is easy to see where everything should go without the stylistic elements getting in the way.

Wireframe layouts are an effective tool for creating a first draft of the media product also known as a **prototype**. As all the different elements of a media product are brought together on a wireframe layout, it is very effective for testing out how a user might access and use those different elements. A 'home' button may be in the wrong place, for example, and by using a wireframe layout it may become clear that it needs moving or that the shape of it needs to be changed.

To improve the effectiveness of wireframe layouts, you should ensure that they are clear, straightforward to understand and take notice of the conventions of the media products they are based on. Unlike a visualisation diagram, a wireframe layout is a guide to the structure of a product rather than a detailed representation of what the final product should look like.

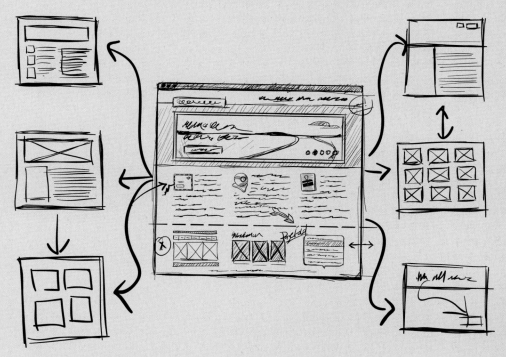

Figure 1.31: Hand drawn wireframes. What do you think could be added to these?

Let's get creative!

Pick a real media example of any of the products listed below:

- DVD cover
- music video
- app for tablet
- video game.
- magazine front cover

1 Create a pre-production plan that outlines what planning documents would have been used to plan the product and why.

2 Draw a flow chart that shows what order the planning documents may have been created in.

3.4 The legal issues that affect media

A key part of pre-production planning is to know what legal issues may arise, both during and after a media product has been created. If you do not spot and understand the potential legal issues, you could find some expensive and difficult problems arise later down the line. In some cases this could mean that your media product has to be cancelled altogether.

Legal considerations to protect individuals

When you work in a media organisation, there are many legal issues that can apply to you, your working practices and the content of media products you are making. Table 1.21 shows the legal considerations to protect individuals and how they are complied with.

Table 1.21: Legal considerations to protect individuals

Purpose of legal consideration	Who/what does it affect?	Example	How to comply with the legal consideration
Privacy and permissions: Privacy law protects people's private lives. **Permission** should be given by the person whose photo/story/work is being used in a media product.	Any media product that uses footage, photographs or other details about people or private locations.	In 2019 Facebook was required by the US Federal Trade Commission to pay a $5 billion penalty and change its privacy restrictions. It had told its users that they could control how their personal information could be shared and this was not the case.	Users' security information and details should not be shared with third parties without permission.
Defamation: **Defamation** is a spoken or written statement that is both false and hurtful to the person's reputation.	Any media product that makes statements about a person, their behaviour or their character.	The *Mail on Sunday* newspaper paid damages and apologised to Prince Harry for saying that Harry had snubbed the Royal Marines and ignored correspondence from a former British Military Chief while he was still supposed to be serving. Prince Harry donated the money to the Invictus Games.	The newspaper should have checked their facts for accuracy, written that this situation had 'allegedly' happened or not reported on it at all if they did not have evidence to back up their statements.
Data protection: Data protection is the right a person has to know how their data will be used, stored and shared.	Media products such as websites that have interactive forms on them, subscription services or apps that hold people's personal data.	The taxi app Uber had the data of millions of both driver and user accounts hacked in 2016 due to poor app information security. Instead of reporting it, Uber paid the hacker £100 000 to keep quiet and none of the people whose personal data was leaked were told. They were then found out and Uber US was fined $148 million, while Uber Europe was fined £385 000.	The app needed to have stronger information security when it was designed. Once a data leak had been identified, Uber should have informed their customers and drivers immediately.

Privacy and permissions

There are several legal considerations regarding privacy and permissions, depending on the situation and the filming or photography required.

- **Rights for recording images/taking photographs in public places:** It is legal to record images or take photographs in public places of people, objects and buildings without permission. However, you also have no control over people going about their business. This may sometimes prove difficult because a public place may well be busy and difficult to film in, and when filming you are not allowed to cause an obstruction. A film company may request for a public area to be closed off while they film in that location. They may use **extras** instead of the public to make the scene look busy, because then they can control what the people say and do. It is legal to take photos or footage of celebrities when they are in public without permission, which is what many independent photographers (the paparazzi) do. These photos are then sold on to media outlets.

Figure 1.32: Why do you think newspapers pay such large amounts for paparazzi photos?

- **Permissions for recording images/taking photographs on private property:** Many places that may seem like they are public are in fact private property, and because of this you will need permission to film or take photographs there. Examples include schools, public transport, libraries and council-owned parks. Commercial (paid for) photographers and professional film crews will need permission to take photos here. For example, permission was not required from everyone in the photo of Central Park in New York (Figure 1.33), but the photographer had to apply for approval from the Central Park Conservancy and the Mayor's Office of Media and Entertainment.

Figure 1.33: What do you think would have happened if the photographer had not applied for approval?

Any other private property such as a house, office building, restaurant or shopping centre will also require permission from the owner before filming or photography can take place. This may also mean paying the owner or landlord a fee.

- **Permissions for publishing and commercial use of images and photographs taken:** If you are taking photos or video specifically of actors or models, then an agreement must be made with them. A model release form should be signed that establishes where and how the images will be used along with any payment the model will receive.

Although it is the photographer who 'owns' the photos they have taken, a model can try to prevent unauthorised publication of images if no model release form has been signed. Using any image in a media product usually requires permission from the owner of the image and may also include payment for the use of it.

- **Harassment and invasion of privacy:** On occasion photographers or film crews can become too persistent and aggressive, which may be viewed as harassment. There have been instances of both celebrities and members of the public making complaints about individual photographers or filmmakers who have taken their desire for the best or most shocking photo too far and have invaded the personal space of the person they are taking photos of. Taking photos and video footage of private property from a public place (such as a street or a field) is allowed, but the people within the private property have a reasonable right to privacy, so the footage must not invade that. It is not acceptable, for example, to stand on a ladder on a public pavement with a camera with a huge zoom lens taking photos through somebody's kitchen window. For similar reasons, along with health and safety concerns, there are now also rules regarding where and how drone footage can be taken in public areas.

Defamation

There are two types of defamatory statements that can be made about a person:

- **Libel:** When a false and hurtful comment about a person is written and then published, leading to their reputation being damaged or them being avoided or subject to hatred. This could be on a website, in a news article, in a book or even on social media.

- **Slander:** When the damaging comments are spoken publicly about the person, or to someone else who then makes those comments public, exposing that person to ridicule or disrespect. The impact of a defamatory statement can prove very costly for both the person defamed and the media producers who are to blame. Someone who has been defamed may find that they are not able to do their job properly or may not be able to work in the industry anymore. They may be shunned by their family, friends or local community. It can be very damaging.

If you defame someone, you could be taken to court, or need to pay a settlement of money by way of an apology. You may also be required to apologise publicly or explain that the defamatory statements were false.

For example, it might not be defamatory to say that the actress Gal Gadot (*Wonder Woman*, 1984) cannot sing and that she sometimes mimes to songs, even though it may be untrue. Gal Gadot is not well-known as a singer and it would not hurt her reputation, nor would she be ridiculed by the publication of that information. However, if the same thing was said about well-known singer Demi Lovato, it might be very different as her reputation as an excellent singer who sings all her own songs is key to her success.

Data protection

Digital technology and the explosion of social media platforms led to people sharing their data more than ever before and often they did not know who was using their data and what it was being used for. Since the Data Protection Act was introduced and then updated with the General Data Protection Regulation in 2018, we have been given more rights in the collection, use and storage of our own personal data.

Data protection gives you control over your personal data and how it is used, so that you know where and when it is being accessed and shared. This means that media companies can no longer keep data that they do not need or is irrelevant, and they cannot keep data for long periods of time if it is not being regularly used. Your data also cannot be shared with other companies without your permission.

However, media organisations can use personal data when producing news articles if there is public interest in doing so. They cannot provide so much data that the person's privacy could be invaded though, and this can be a difficult balancing act. It must, of course, also be accurate.

For example, if you printed the address and telephone number of a man convicted of several burglaries around a town in an article in the local newspaper, this could result in members of the public visiting his house or calling his family, which would not be appropriate and is an invasion of his privacy.

Media producers need to be careful about how they obtain the information in the first place. If they take the information without consent, then this is a criminal offence that can come with a fine. This includes lying or deception, phone or email hacking and going undercover.

Intellectual property rights

Intellectual property rights are those we are given over our ideas and creations that we have in our minds. It can be quite a difficult concept to prove sometimes, to make sure that your idea is your own and has not been accidentally or subconsciously borrowed from someone else.

Protecting intellectual property (IP)

There are several different pieces of legislation that help people to register their ideas so that IP rights are respected and protected, and to help the victim if ideas are copied. There is also legislation to guide you when using artwork, audio and video assets so that you properly credit the creator. Table 1.22 outlines the different legislation that protects IP.

Table 1.22: Protecting IP

Purpose of legislation	Who/what does it affect?	Example	How to respect IP rights
Copyright: A law which gives the creator of any media form the exclusive rights to it, meaning it can only be copied, shared or edited with their permission.	Any media product that contains images, sound, video, logos or anything else that has not been created by the designers/creatives themselves.	In 2021, a voice-over actor filed a legal complaint over TikTok using her voice, without her knowledge or permission, for its 'text to speech' feature used in the US version of the video-based app. TikTok changed the voice just weeks later.	TikTok should have commissioned their own voice-over actor to record the words and phrases they needed, or they could have contacted the actor to ask for her permission to use her voice recordings.
Patent: A licence that grants exclusive rights to the creator for a design idea, process or an invention.	Anyone that has a design idea that they want to keep to themselves for creative advantage so that others cannot use it would need to apply for a patent.	Facebook has a patent for 'dynamically providing a news feed about a user of a social network' so technically no other company can do this.	Companies can find their own ways of providing similar media services or will need to come up with their own designs.
Trademark: A phrase, individual words, logo or symbol that is protected because it is registered as representing a specific business, brand or product.	Any media business that wishes to make sure no one can copy their logo, campaign name or brand name. They will be able to use the ® symbol after the word or phrase once registered. The ™ sign is for unregistered trademarks.	Kylie Jenner owns 130 trademarks including 'Kylie Museum' and 'Kylie Con'. Between them, the Kardashians have over 700 trademarks to stop others copying them.	Once a word or phrase has been registered as a trademark, it cannot be used by anyone else unless it is for informational use or comparison between products and services.

Using copyrighted materials

When creative work is produced, you or your business automatically holds the copyright for it, meaning that your IP is protected from those who wish to copy it. There is no application process or fee to pay. You can then decide whether you want to allow your product to be rented, sold or used as well as how you want to be credited or acknowledged for being the creator. Most creative works are protected for the life of the author, plus 70 years. When copyright expires, the work becomes freely available to the public to use, edit and even sell.

If a business is found guilty of copyright infringement, the implications can be quite severe. In other words, breaking copyright law can have consequences like large fines and even prison sentences.

If you are using creative material, you always need to know whether the work you are using is copyrighted. Once you have found out who the material belongs to, you must ask for and receive permission to use it. This can come at a price or require you to credit the original creator.

Finding the original creator of an asset can be difficult, so there are other methods that media organisations use to ensure that they do not accidentally violate copyright law.

- **Creative Commons (CC) licences:** Some creators release their work under a CC licence, meaning you can use their work for free if you follow their requirements. There are different levels of CC licence with different requirements, including: **attribution**, **share alike**, no **derivative works** and **non-commercial**.

  For example, if a festival banner was to be made and one of the graphics is a hand drawn tent then the banner would be the derivative work and the tent would be the copyrighted image. CC licences work around the world and you can search for CC content using Google, Flickr and Jamendo through the CC website. Wikipedia also has a source of CC material called Wikimedia Commons, so there are many options to choose from and lots of images, sounds, videos and other assets available for free.

- **Fair dealing:** There are instances when you can use normally copyrighted creative material without infringing copyright law. This is called fair dealing and refers to content that is used for research and individual private study, being reviewed or quoted, and in news reporting.

It also relates to work that is used to illustrate points in education, so copyrighted material can be used by teachers to a certain extent. Fair dealing also extends to parody, caricature and pastiche. These are terms that relate to developing, imitating, exaggerating or enhancing material. Parody and caricature are usually used to be humorous, but pastiche could be an imitation done to bring the work to a new audience or to demonstrate a particular style.

One example of this is comic fan fiction where artwork is created by fans of the genre to imitate the style of their favourite comic books, as shown in Figure 1.34. While creating and sharing fan fiction artwork online is acceptable, it would breach copyright of the original comic artist to print out and sell fan fiction artwork in any way.

- **Permissions, fees and licences:** There are other ways to buy the rights to copyrighted materials. One option is to buy individual images from a stock image library such as iStock, which range in price depending on the content and dimensions of the asset. To learn more about the two main types of stock library image licence, see Unit R094, Topic Area 2, 'Stock library images'.

Figure 1.34: How do you think the copyright holders of comic artwork feel about fan fiction?

Another option is to have a subscription with an image library such as Getty Images or Shutterstock and pay monthly or per batch of images. Finally, another option is to visit copyright-free image sites such as Pixabay and Unsplash which have varying levels of free use including free commercial use with no attribution or crediting of the creator being required.

- **Watermarks and symbols:** Watermarks are translucent logos, stamps or other symbols that are superimposed onto digital images and photographs so that when they are downloaded for free from the internet without a licence or permission, the image cannot be used effectively. To use a non-watermarked version, you would have to pay to download it, or be granted permission to use it. On occasion, during planning, watermarked versions of images may be used for mock-ups, with the paid-for versions being purchased before the final product is made and distributed.

Regulation, certification and classification

Many areas of both traditional and new media are regulated by media law and others are expected to adhere to published guidelines and codes of conduct. Regulations are essentially the rules that are enforced by law and the purpose of them is to restrict, develop or shape the way the media works.

The reason that regulation exists is to protect the consumers of media products and to ensure that unsuitable or inappropriate material does not reach audiences. There are key organisations that are responsible for regulation of the media industry along with several systems to classify and certificate media products.

Organisations responsible for regulation

There are two key organisations responsible for regulation in the UK, the Advertising Standards Authority (ASA) and the Office for Communications (Ofcom).

Advertising Standards Authority (ASA)

The ASA is the independent regulator for the advertising industry across all types of media in the UK. It is funded by the advertising industry but remains separate from it. The ASA is responsible for ensuring that advertisers follow the rules laid out in the Advertising Codes, which are documents written by the Committee of Advertising Practice (CAP).

The Advertising Codes are 22 standards relating to aspects including privacy, children, harm and offence, and misleading advertising. The ASA has been ensuring advertisers adhere to these codes for over 50 years and to date have resolved over 36 300 complaints related to nearly 23 000 adverts.

Any person or organisation can make a complaint to the ASA about an advert they have seen. The ASA will investigate and take action to ban or amend adverts that they believe are harmful, misleading, irresponsible or offensive. They also monitor the adverts running to make sure they are following the rules. The American equivalent is the American Advertising Federation.

There are different processes for print/online adverts and broadcast adverts, but both are regulated against the same Advertising Codes. The flow charts in Figure 1.35, on the next page, show the processes for both print/online and broadcast adverts.

The impact of the regulation standards on advert production is clear at all stages of planning, production and distribution. Even once you have successfully created and distributed a product there is always the possibility that a complaint could come from a member of the public and be upheld.

Those in senior media production roles have a responsibility to check that the adverts being produced adhere to the codes to ensure that their client does not receive negative publicity from having an advert banned. In extreme cases the advertiser would be referred to the local government authority department, Trading Standards, where a financial penalty or even imprisonment can be imposed by a court.

The Office of Communications (Ofcom)

Ofcom is the regulatory body for the broadcasting industry in the UK. Its role is to uphold the Ofcom Broadcasting Code, a set of rules to be followed for the broadcast of all programmes on TV, radio, on demand services and UK established video-sharing platforms.

When making a programme, you have a responsibility to follow the code to ensure that it:

- is scheduled properly and correct information is provided about it to protect those under 18

- meets the standards for protection from harmful or offensive material

- does not incite crime or disorder

- is impartial and accurate when containing news in whatever form

- does not treat individuals or organisations unfairly or unjustly

- does not infringe privacy rights

- clearly indicates when advertising is taking place.

Print and online advertising versus broadcast advertising

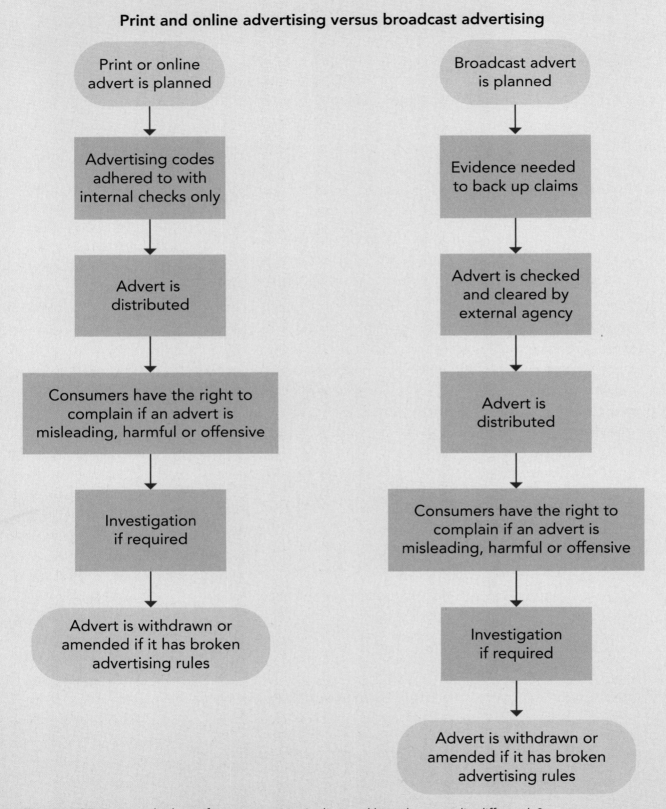

Figure 1.35: Do you think it is fair to treat print/online and broadcast media differently?

Once a programme has been broadcast, any individual or organisation can make a complaint about it, as can any of the people who are the subject of the programme. A complaint can be made online, by phone or by post. All complaints are assessed, but not all will be investigated. For example, on 22 April 2021 Ofcom received 107 complaints about misleading material in the breakfast TV show *Lorraine*. It was deemed by Ofcom that these complaints did not raise issues warranting investigation.

Once an investigation has happened, a decision is made and published on Ofcom's public website that either:

- the company has already resolved the issue
- the complaint is to be upheld because the code has not been properly adhered to
- the programme is in direct breach of specific points in the broadcasting code, or
- the complaint is not upheld.

If a broadcaster continues to break the rules or breaks a rule in a serious or reckless way, Ofcom has legal powers to impose sanctions or consequences, including:

- an order not to repeat the programme or content
- broadcast of a statement to correct the information presented or a statement of Ofcom's findings
- financial penalties
- shortening, suspending or taking away completely the channel or station's licence to broadcast.

The impact of the Ofcom broadcasting code on media production is far-reaching. Creatives, technical staff and those in senior roles all need to be aware of it right up to the point that the programme is broadcast. Even then, there could be a possibility that there will be complaints.

Greener Technology Ltd and Ofcom

In October 2019, Ofcom fined Greener Technology Ltd £25 000. Its TV channel BEN TV did not comply with their broadcasting rules.

On 28 January 2018, BEN TV broadcast a programme featuring footage from televangelist Peter Popoff's religious services. In it there were frequent invitations for viewers to order 'free miracle spring water' and several testimonies from people who claimed, or strongly implied, that using the water had cured serious illnesses, including cancer.

Figure 1.36: Free 'miracle spring water' was offered in the TV broadcast

Ofcom decided that the claims had the potential to cause harm to members of the audience who may believe that 'miracle spring water' alone was enough to cure their health conditions and that it was unnecessary to rely on, or continue receiving, medical treatment by doctors.

Ofcom also told Greener Technology Ltd to not repeat the programme.

Check your understanding

1   What claims were being made on the TV programme?

2   What was Ofcom's issue with the claims?

3   Why do you think that Ofcom believed these claims could cause harm?

4   What impact do you think the fine and not being able to broadcast the programme again might have on the TV channel?

Classification systems and certifications

Classification is the process of assigning specific age ratings to films, TV shows, video games and other digital products that advise the audience who the product is suitable for. As well as the age rating or certification itself, the classification will also include specific content advice to help consumers decide what is right for them to watch and what they may wish to stay away from.

Classification certificates need to be displayed on the product and promotional materials so that it is clear what classification the product has been given. Content providers and streamers, such as Netflix and Amazon, also use these classifications to help inform their users.

Factoring classification and certification into planning a media product is key, as the impact of a delay to receiving the certificate could also mean a delay to the release of the product, or even mean it is not released at all. For example, all films shown in the UK must have an age rating by law, and it is against the law to sell DVDs or digital video without one.

British Board of Film Classification (BBFC)

The BBFC was created in 1912 and is an independent, not-for-profit regulator providing classification and labelling systems for media content that is shown in the UK including:

- films
- music videos
- TV shows.
- non-playable video content within video games
- other online digital content

Films must be submitted to the BBFC for analysis before they can be distributed to cinemas. It is the responsibility of the compliance officers to view the content and make decisions. Films can be submitted from all over the world because the BBFC relates to any content being shown in the UK.

Compliance officers make notes as they are watching and create a report that will recommend a specific age rating. These recommendations are based on the issues outlined in Figure 1.37.

Issues to look for

- General theme
- Plot
- Bad or offensive language
- Sex
- Discrimination
- Horror
- Nudity

- Dangerous behaviour
- Violence
- Drug references
- Key shots and camera angles
- Key scenes, moments and timings
- Characters

Figure 1.37: Do you think these issues should be judged in an order of importance?

It is possible to submit your film and ask for a specific age rating. Compliance officers may decide that a higher age rating is needed, or they could outline some cuts to bring it back to the age rating requested.

The age rating is used on the product and packaging as well as on all promotional materials, so certification must be received once the product has been finished, but before it is distributed. Figure 1.38 shows the possible age ratings that can be attributed to products.

U	Suitable for all
PG	Parental guidance
12A	Cinema release suitable for 12 years and over
12	Video release suitable for 12 years and over
15	Suitable only for 15 years and over
18	Suitable only for adults
R18	Adult works for licensed premises only

Figure 1.38: Would you add any more age ratings? Why?

Pan European Game Information (PEGI)

The role of PEGI is to provide clear age classifications for video games in 38 European countries. It is an independent, not-for-profit company that provides an age rating system that can be applied and checked on behalf of PEGI in each participating country.

In the same way that BBFC classifications outline the suitability of films and videos for audiences, PEGI certification confirms that a game is appropriate for players of a particular age group. It provides information and guidance on the content. The PEGI classification system is not based on how easy or complex the game is to play; it is based on the suitability of the content for users, as defined by the PEGI Code of Conduct.

PEGI ratings can be applied for before the game is released, or can be verified afterwards. It is the responsibility of the media organisation applying to be transparent and honest with the information supplied.

Figure 1.39 shows the different aspects taken into consideration.

Suitability aspects

- General theme
- Plot/narrative
- Bad or offensive language
- Sex and/or nudity
- Discrimination
- Frightening content (sound and images)
- Gambling
- In-game purchases
- Dangerous behaviour
- Violence
- Use of tobacco, alcohol, drugs
- Locations
- Characters

Figure 1.39: Which of these do you think comes up the most in video games?

PEGI has an online rating system that analyses the responses and automatically determines a provisional age rating for the game. The PEGI administrators then receive the game itself and review it alongside the provisional age rating given. Depending on how many different aspects are identified, the number of instances and the nature of each one, the original rating will be approved or altered, and a licence is given to the media production company along with the appropriate certificate for use on the product, packaging and in promotional materials.

Along with a number that relates to the age of the suitable audience, PEGI also issues content descriptors which are small logos showing what is present in the video game. This gives consumers a quick and handy at-a-glance guide to the video game content. These logos are shown in Figure 1.40 and described in Table 1.23.

Figure 1.40: Why do you think the BBFC classifications and PEGI age labels are different?

Table 1.23: PEGI age suitability labels

Age suitability labels
3 – Content is considered suitable for all age groups
7 – Scenes or sounds may frighten younger children
12 – Non-realistic violence, bad language must be mild
16 – Real-life depictions of violence or sex, bad language
18 – Adult classification

Over to you!   2

Visit the 'Coming Soon' or 'In Theatres' section of the Internet Movie Database website and choose a trailer for a film that is a PG or 12A.

1   Watch the trailer and use the BBFC issues in Figure 1.37 to identify why you think the trailer has been given a PG or 12A certificate.

2   Why do you think it is important to have classification and certification of media products? Use examples of films that you have seen in your answer.

Health and safety

When working in the media industry, you need to be able to feel safe doing your job. One of the main ways to ensure that everyone involved in a project stays fit, healthy and safe is to plan proper health and safety controls in all phases of a project.

Filmmaker Steven Spielberg has said of the importance of health and safety in the media industry that, 'No movie is worth dying for,' and that, 'If something isn't safe, it's the right and responsibility of every actor or crew member to yell, "Cut!"' Health and safety is the responsibility of every single person in the media industry and a great deal of it is about using common sense and taking care.

Assessing risk and identifying hazards is key to keeping everyone safe. The best way to minimise accidents is to plan for their possibility, and to have **health and safety mitigations** in place.

Common risks and hazards that can be found in media production, along with actions that can be taken to mitigate these risks, are outlined in Table 1.24.

Table 1.24: Media production risk assessment

Hazard	Risk: Who and how	Action to mitigate risk
Heavy equipment	Equipment falling over and injuring someone, or straining someone's back through lifting	Ensure all heavy equipment is checked so that it is secure and that it is lifted by machinery or by more than one person. Manual handling training.
Set/location	Falling set; injury from using set incorrectly; trip/slip/fall	Set needs to be built securely, inspected and everyone using it needs to know the procedures for use. Location recce should be completed to identify any specific risks.
Spillages on floor or near equipment	People may fall over on slippery surfaces	Ensure food and drinks are not near to the equipment and are kept in designated areas.
Electrical equipment and systems	Overheating; short circuiting if left on too long or over-used; electric shock	Ensure appliances are turned off when not in use. All equipment safety checked.
Cables and plug sockets	Trip; electrical fire; electric shock	Cables need to be tidy, taped to the floor or held by someone.
Props, costumes	Trip; overheating; discomfort; sickness; tiredness	If costumes are heavy or hot, appropriate cooling sources are needed. Actors may also need help to move around.

Table 1.24: Continued

Hazard	Risk: Who and how	Action to mitigate risk
Computers	Eye strain; headaches; mental fatigue; tiredness; heightened stress levels	Take regular breaks, wear glasses if necessary and limit hours of work.
Unsuitable clothing and footwear	Trips; falls; overheating; getting too cold; back pain; sore feet	Wear appropriate clothing for the job being undertaken, e.g. trainers, t-shirt, layers or head wear.
The public	Getting in the way of actors, crew or equipment; trips/falls	Ensure members of the public are either kept away from the area or are monitored at all times.
Long working hours	Tiredness; mental fatigue; exhaustion; headaches	Hours required should be realistic and reasonable. Ensure adequate food and breaks. No one should be required to drive or operate complex machinery while tired.
Weather: heatwave, storms, snow, ice, lightning, changeable conditions	Sunburn; heatstroke; dehydration; damage to equipment making it unsafe	Check the weather forecast; suitable clothing; plan breaks, food and drinks; limit exposure to extreme conditions; hats, sunglasses, water, sunscreen.
Vehicles	Injury to cast or crew; accident; injury to public	Ensure appropriate licences are held, that the Highway Code is adhered to and that there is appropriate insurance.
Animals	Attack by animal – bite, scratch, sting; allergic reaction; stress or anxiety	Having an animal expert present; careful choice of animals; safety briefing; first aid; evacuation of venue if needed.
Heights	Fall from a height; struck by falling objects; fear of heights; getting stuck	Those working at height should be experienced, competent and willing. Equipment should be inspected, secured and maintained. Use personal protective equipment such as harnesses and hard hats.

To spot and assess health and safety risks and hazards, all media organisations should have in place the following planning documents, roles and procedures:

- A **health and safety policy** which outlines the risks, hazards and processes for dealing with them.

- A **risk assessment** which outlines the potential risks and hazards in a particular situation and details the mitigations that can be put in place to protect against them. The risk assessment would usually include a date, along with the name of the person responsible for completing it. This is to ensure that the information is up-to-date, and so that it is clear who can provide further information regarding risk factors.

- **Call sheets** sent out to all film/TV/radio/video/photo shoot cast and crew. These let everyone know when and where they will be needed and will include safety notes.

- A competent **health and safety officer** who knows what the risks are in the environment they work in and can be approached for advice and guidance.

- **Health and safety training** provided to everyone on the project to ensure that they are able to carry out their tasks safely and are aware of the health and safety risks. This includes knowing what they should and should not do when carrying out their activities.

- **Equipment and site inspections** by the health and safety officer to check that the activities being completed and the equipment being used are safe and appropriate.

- A designated **first aid representative or medic** available on location and in all places of work.

- **Permission from all locations** being filmed in to use the sites.

- **Location recces** should be carried out for all filming locations to assess their suitability for use and any health and safety risks. The information gathered is helpful for the whole production team. They inform the creative team what they are working with and enable them to plan shot types, camera angles, props, costumes and scenes. They help the production and technical teams to schedule what days and times are best for filming, and what equipment will be needed for lighting and sound. They also help to know whether any permits are required, to get any extra insurance or health and safety training needed for that location, and to plan for catering and comfort of cast and crew.

Stretch

A new video game, based in the Austrian Alps, will digitise real footage of the mountains and turn them into animated location backgrounds in the video game itself. The footage will be shot with a drone, a helicopter, a glider and some point of view shots from skiers/snowboarders too.

Create a detailed location recce and health and safety risk assessment for the filming of the footage, on location in Austria.

Annotate both documents to justify the information you have included.

Review your learning

Test your knowledge

1   Identify which planning documents would be most suitable for use when planning:

   a   a music video   **b**   a promotional flyer   **c**   a website.

2   Explain the ways in which a graphic designer could ensure that they did not infringe upon IP rights.

3   Discuss the importance of regulation, classification and certification in the media industry.

4   Create a health and safety document that demonstrates your knowledge of the potential risks to filming a documentary in your school.

What have you learnt?

	See section
• Work planning.	3.1
• Documents used to support ideas generation.	3.2
• Documents used to design and plan media products.	3.3
• The legal issues that affect media.	3.4

Distribution considerations

Let's get started

Many people enjoy going to the cinema. How do you think films get to the cinema to be viewed by an audience?

What other media products might a cinema use?

Figure 1.41: Visiting a cinema is just one of the ways that an audience can access a film

What will you learn?

- Distribution platforms and media to reach audiences.
- Properties and formats of media files.

Once you have made and finalised a media product, it then needs to be distributed. Distribution is the method of sending out a media product to the intended audience(s) through a particular platform and type of media. You might find that a media product is distributed across several platforms so that audiences can access it in different ways.

Before you can make any decisions about how your product will be distributed, there are lots of things to think about. These are called distribution considerations. Some of these distribution considerations relate to platforms, file formats, **resolution** and product quality.

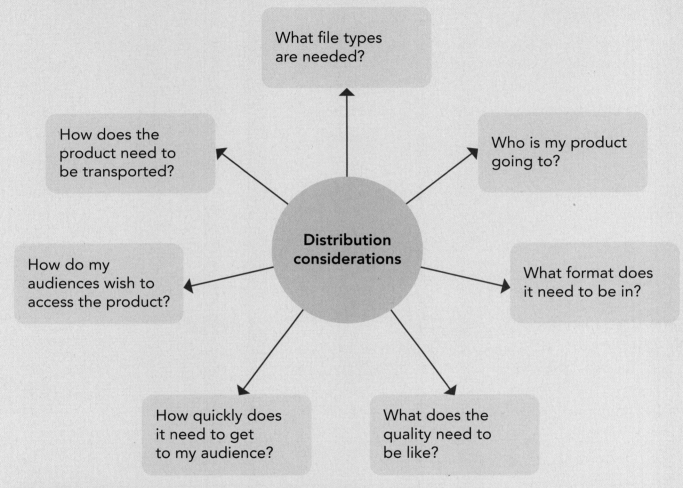

Figure 1.42: Which of these considerations do you think is most important?

4.1 Distribution platforms and media to reach audiences

There are so many distribution options in the modern media industry, that it can be difficult to choose the most appropriate one for a particular audience. Many projects will require more than one distribution platform, as the different characteristics of each platform will offer opportunities and limitations for getting the media product out to its audience. To make the right choice you need to know what these are, and the advantages and disadvantages of each platform and physical media type.

Online platforms

Online platforms are generally cheaper than others and take less physical organisation of equipment. Media products can often be distributed more quickly online. If you need to update or amend a media product, it is much easier and cheaper to amend an online product and upload an updated version. However, there is a lack of control over who sees the product and when. Interaction is also not guaranteed and is difficult to measure.

There are three main types of online platform: apps, multimedia and web. The following three sections discuss the characteristics, examples and advantages/disadvantages of each type of online platform.

Apps

Characteristics: Downloadable from an app store and accessed instantly from mobile devices. They are updated frequently via the internet. Files can be embedded in the app.

Example: A new film trailer could be uploaded to the YouTube app or a new song could be uploaded to the YouTube Music app. This could then be shared via Facebook, another distribution app.

Figure 1.43: A song may be distributed in several different ways. How many can you think of?

Table 1.25: App platform advantages and disadvantages

Advantages	Disadvantages
• Quick and easy to update • Potentially free to access • Users can watch/interact anywhere • Only requires phone or tablet • Easy to interact with	• Consumers must have the app downloaded to get the content • Limited file sizes • Limited to app shape and structure • Likely to need internet to access content

Multimedia

Characteristics: Multimedia spaces are used to make, share and view content. They are delivered digitally, directly to the audience. They are digital packages of audio, video, text and images.

Example: Podcasts and blogs that are interactive with audio content, text and potentially embedded links. Content such as a newsletter or educational presentation could be uploaded onto a blog.

Table 1.26: Multimedia platform advantages and disadvantages

Advantages	Disadvantages
• Allows a range of content • Great interactivity	• Content tends to need sending to a consumer before they can access it, or a link needs to be sent • May also need the internet for external links

Web

Characteristics: Websites can have content easily embedded for its audiences to access. They can show a combination of audio, video, text and images and allow live content to be streamed too.

Example: Static and moving adverts can be embedded alongside other media content in websites to deliver promotional marketing messages to interested audiences.

Table 1.27: Web platform advantages and disadvantages

Advantages	Disadvantages
• Easy to access using the internet • Can be searched for using a search engine • Moving content is easy to embed • Quick to upload and update	• Specific sizes and dimensions often needed • Requires the internet • Can get lost among all the other web content • May require coding • Will not take larger file sizes and file types are restricted

Physical platforms

There are four main types of physical platforms: computer, interactive TV, kiosks and mobile devices. The following four sections discuss the characteristics, examples and advantages/disadvantages of each type of physical platform.

Computer

Characteristics: Can be used to run video, audio, multimedia products, eBooks and games independently or in a network.

Example: A cinema may use a computer to play the film that is then projected digitally onto the screen.

Table 1.28: Computer platform advantages and disadvantages

Advantages	Disadvantages
• Can show products with complex levels of interactivity • Will show most media products • Internet not always needed • Powerful with few limits to file sizes and types • Quantities, views and interactivity of users can all be monitored	• Expensive product to buy so not all members of the target audience will have one • Not always portable • Relies on being set up properly

Interactive TV

Characteristics: Streams and can save downloadable audio and video content, as well as video games.

Example: A television and film streaming provider such as Disney+ uses interactive TVs for customers to view content directly and to advertise other potential programmes of interest to the target audience.

Table 1.29: Interactive TV platform advantages and disadvantages

Advantages	Disadvantages
• Access to many different apps and channels • Highly interactive, content is trackable and searchable • Speed of delivery • Content can be sent directly to the interactive TV via the internet • Content usually matched to target audience preferences	• Not portable • Too much choice so no guarantee product will be seen • Expensive to buy so not everyone has one

Kiosks

Characteristics: A static product that can show an interactive multimedia presentation, video or game. Usually used independently or as part of a small network. Sometimes requires the internet to access content.

Example: A museum may use a kiosk to enhance the information they can provide on their artefacts. This could offer 3D sketches of what buildings or objects may have looked like, video and sound enhancements or quizzes.

Figure 1.44: Where else might kiosks like this be useful?

Table 1.30: Kiosk platform advantages and disadvantages

Advantages	Disadvantages
• Can be set up in restaurants, museums, offices, banks, etc. • Easy for consumers to use • Highly interactive • Can process many file types • Can have multiple users	• Target audience is limited to people who physically go to the kiosk to look at the product • Generally not portable • Often limited in what it can present • Needs maintenance • May not have speakers

Mobile devices

Characteristics: Applies to tablets, mobiles and even watches. Allow a range of digital content to be downloaded or accessed through the internet or via Bluetooth.

Example: An eBook could be downloaded onto a mobile device either through an app or as a PDF file.

Table 1.31: Mobile device platform advantages and disadvantages

Advantages	Disadvantages
• Mass audiences • Fast-moving technology • Highly interactive	• Huge competition • Relies on Bluetooth/internet • Can have limited memory

Table 1.31: Continued

Advantages	Disadvantages
• Portable • Come with accessories such as headphones for sound • Quick distribution • Good range of compatible file types	• Android/Mac operating systems require different setup/content

Stretch

Your company has been asked to design, create and distribute a voucher booklet to families. It contains money-off coupons for attractions and theme parks around the country.

The voucher booklet has been created. The distribution is your responsibility.

Write a detailed distribution plan that explains which platforms should be used and why. Your plan should explain who each form of distribution is targeting and how it will be successful.

Physical media

You also have a choice of physical media to distribute on, which can be used with both physical and online platforms, or on their own. There are three main types of physical media: CD/DVD, memory stick and paper based. The following three sections discuss the characteristics, examples and advantages/disadvantages of each type of physical media.

CD and DVD

Characteristics: A small, plastic, easily transportable disc that can be played in a computer, DVD player, games console or CD player. Content is downloaded (burnt) directly onto the surface of the disc so it can be read in a player.

Figure 1.45: What do you think are the advantages of distributing an interactive presentation on USB?

Example: A TV production company may release a whole series of programmes on a collection of DVDs as a box set, to be watched at a time convenient for the consumer.

Meanwhile an interactive presentation may be sent on a USB or CD and be downloaded onto a computer as well as being available on a website.

Table 1.32: CD/DVD media advantages and disadvantages

Advantages	Disadvantages
• Audiences can keep a physical copy and access it over and over again • Does not rely on the internet • Can be sent directly to target audience as well as into shops	• Costly to produce • Takes time to make • Fixed size and space for content, which also cannot be updated or edited once on the disc • Requires a player • Flimsy and fragile

Memory stick

Characteristics: A type of removable USB device that can connect to computers and TVs. They store different amounts of data depending on the size of the memory on the stick.

Example: The Amazon Fire TV Stick connects a TV with a streaming player that accesses online streaming content. It does not hold the programmes themselves on the stick; instead, it includes the player and the files needed to access online content.

Figure 1.46: What are the disadvantages of distributing through an Amazon Fire TV Stick?

Table 1.33: Memory stick media advantages and disadvantages

Advantages	Disadvantages
• Small, therefore easy to transport (portable) • Physical copy, so no worry that it will be taken away • Does not necessarily rely on internet • Often has large amounts of memory • Allows the user to share and transfer pictures, sound, video and other data	• Requires a computer or TV to work • File compatibility can be a problem • Content can be erased or overwritten • Easily lost or broken

Paper based

Characteristics: The oldest and most traditional physical media form. Paper based media products can be printed and distributed by hand or by vehicle to their location. Includes posters, newsletters and other printed content.

Example: A series of Adshel posters, which are large sheets that are posted onto the side of a bus, the walls of bus shelters and the ends of bus stops.

Table 1.34: Paper based media advantages and disadvantages

Advantages	Disadvantages
• Physical copies have visual impact • Print quality • Professional looking • Can be placed in a range of locations	• Expensive to produce • Often some wastage • Can be easily damaged • Costly to transport and get to the audience • Can be difficult to track the impact of print adverts

Over to you!   1

Choose the most appropriate distribution platforms and/or media for each of these media products:

a   a new interactive multimedia product that can be used to both buy new clothes and to donate clothes to charity

b   a video game that can be played on a range of platforms

c   an informational poster about how to ride an e-bike.

4.2 Properties and formats of media files

Once you have finished a media product and decided what distribution platforms and/or media the product will be released on, you will then be able to select the appropriate media files to support the distribution. There are several standard media files that are regularly used in the media industry for static and moving images, and audio. These files have different properties that make them useful depending on what the media product is and how it needs to be distributed.

Static image files

In this section you will look at the properties and formats of static image files.

The properties of digital static image files

The main two properties of static image files that affect the quality of an image are DPI/PPI resolution and **pixel dimension**.

DPI or PPI resolution

The level of detail that is held in an image affects how clear it is. This is called the resolution of an image. The higher the resolution is, the more detail the image will have, therefore the better quality it's likely to be. A lower **pixel** count can result in the image seeming blurry or undefined.

Resolution is usually discussed using the terms **DPI** and PPI. Sometimes they are even used interchangeably, but they are not the same thing.

- **DPI resolution:** DPI stands for 'Dots Per Inch', which describes the number of dots of ink or toner cartridge that are printed onto one inch of an image.

  Printers work by putting lots of tiny dots onto the paper or other material that is being printed onto. The more dots there are, the sharper the detail and the better the overall print quality. The size of the dots never changes between documents printed on the same printer, just how many of them are squeezed into an inch of paper.

  The industry standard for printed documents is a minimum of 300 DPI, because 300 dots are needed per inch to print what humans would see as high-quality printed images. An interesting fact is that there is no manufacturing standard for the size or shape of a printer dot, though they are all quite similar sizes and shapes.

100 DPI 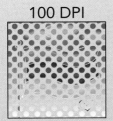 200 DPI 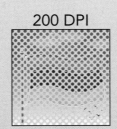 300 DPI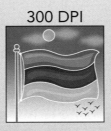

Figure 1.47: Can you think of some media products that are very large and would need a large number of DPI?

- **PPI resolution:** PPI stands for 'Pixels Per Inch' and describes the resolution of a digital image rather than a print image. It refers to the number of the tiny, coloured squares or pixels that can be seen in an inch of a digital image. If an image has a higher PPI it will be higher quality than one with a lower PPI, because it has more pixels in the same space; it will have a higher pixel density.

As an example, the best mobile phone screens have a pixel density of more than 500 PPI and a 50-inch 4K ultra-HD TV screen has a pixel density of only around 90 PPI. The higher the PPI resolution, the larger the file size – but remember, just because you have increased the PPI, this does not mean you will notice any difference on the screen.

If you have a computer screen that only shows pixels at a density of 72 PPI, it does not matter how many more pixels you squash into each inch of the image, the screen can only ever show you 72 PPI. Many computer screens are 72 PPI, so ideally digital products that are to be shown on a computer should have a resolution of around 72 PPI.

Figure 1.48: Why do you think a screen with more pixels is better for your eyes?

Pixel dimension

The pixel dimensions of an image are what we would usually call its size. Instead of using inches or millimetres/centimetres, pixels are generally used for images.

- **Pixel dimensions to inches:** To convert the pixel dimension of an image to inches, you would also need to know the image's PPI. The calculation would be as shown:

> **Pixel height ÷ image PPI = Height in inches**

Example 1

An image that is 100 pixels high by 100 pixels wide with a PPI of 100 will be 1 inch by 1 inch.

$$100 \div 100 = 1$$

Example 2

An image that is 1000 pixels high by 1000 pixels wide with a PPI of 100 will be 10 inches by 10 inches.

$$1000 \div 100 = 10$$

These calculations obviously get more complicated if the PPI changes.

Example 3

An image that is 1000 pixels high by 1000 pixels wide with a PPI of 72 will be 13.8 inches by 13.8 inches.

$$1000 \div 72 = 13.9 \text{ inches}$$

- **Inches to pixel dimensions:** You can do this calculation the other way round to see how many pixels are needed for a digital image of a certain size in inches:

> **Height in inches × image PPI = Pixel height**

Example 4

An image that is 15 inches high by 15 inches wide with a PPI of 100 will be 1500 pixels by 1500 pixels.

- **Pixel dimensions and purpose:** The best way to decide on what dimensions and resolution are best for a static image is to think about the purpose of the media product. An image on a presentation in a kiosk or projected onto a screen would probably need to be of a higher-than-average resolution.

- **Pixel dimensions and quality:** Once you have made an image, you can still change the pixel dimensions. You may need to make it larger or smaller, or even change its shape. For example, a digital graphic that has been created for a film poster may need to be made smaller to fit on a vertical web banner. It is important to keep an eye on the quality of the image when you do this. If you make an image larger without upscaling the PPI, then the same number of pixels per inch will be used – this may not be suitable if the image is then going to be printed as the pixel density will not be enough, leading to pixelation or blur.

Over to you!   2

Practise your dimension and resolution conversion skills using the following media product measurements.

1   What dimensions will an image be that is 635 pixels wide by 425 pixels high with a PPI of 10?

2   An image that is 28 inches high by 32 inches wide with a PPI of 300 will be how many pixels?

3   An image that is 1080 pixels wide by 800 pixels wide has a PPI of 25. What are its dimensions?

Native and standard file formats

Files can be split into two types: **native** image file types and **standard** image file types. These two file types will be explained in the following sections in the context of static image files.

Static image file formats

Static image files are those that contain still images. They will remain still on any media product, rather than moving like video files. The common static image file formats of each type are discussed. Each file type has its own file extension (or shortened name) that is used at the end of the file name to show what type of file it is.

Native file formats

Native file formats are the ones that can only be opened and used by specific or specialist software, often because those file types belong to that software.

If a native file format becomes popular, then it may be that other software providers start the same file format. In that case they start to become more of a standard file format. An example of this is the Photoshop file format, PSD. It was created for use in Adobe Photoshop but can also be used in CorelDRAW, GIMP, PaintShop Pro, Paint.NET and more recently Photopea.

Table 1.35 gives the file extension (in brackets), properties and limitations of some common native static image file formats. See the next two sections in this unit for more information about audio and moving image file formats.

Table 1.35: Native image file formats. See 'file compression' in Unit R094, Topic Area 2 to understand the terms related to compression found in the table, including 'lossless'

Native file format	Properties	Limitations
Adobe Photoshop (.psd)	• Accessible only on graphic design software programs • Large file containing layers of work that can be edited	• Not easily opened without specialist software • Too large and not compatible for use in most media products – Photoshop files need to be exported to image files • When sending someone a Photoshop file, all fonts and images used need sending, too
Adobe Illustrator (.ai)	• Editable vector file • Uncompressed • Often used for digitised hand drawn work such as logos • Easy to view as a PDF	• Can only be edited using specialist software like Adobe Illustrator, Photoshop and CorelDRAW
Affinity Designer (.afdesign)	• Editable vector file • Will not lose quality if enlarged • Mostly used for logos and print media	• When sending someone an Affinity Designer file all linked images and fonts need to be sent too • Needs to be sent as a PDF for sharing and printing
GIMP (.xcf) (GNU Image Manipulation Programme)	• Uncompressed (see 'file compression' in Unit R094, Topic Area 2 to understand this term) • Edit and store layers	• Only openable by using GIMP • Only deals with Red Green Blue (RGB) colour mode
RAW (.dng, .nef, .cr2, etc.)	• Processed directly from a camera • Lossless, no compression used • Often automatically converted to JPEG when downloaded from the camera	• Not easily used by most software • Very large file • File extension relates only to the brand of camera being used

Standard file formats

Standard file formats are common files that can typically be opened without specialist software and are generally what a final media product would be exported to.

Standard static image file formats that can generally be opened and viewed without specialist software. Table 1.36 gives the file extension (in brackets), properties and limitations of some common standard static image file formats. See the next two sections in this unit for more information about audio and moving image file formats.

Table 1.36: Standard static image file formats. See 'file compression' in Unit R094, Topic Area 2 to understand the terms related to compression found in the table, including 'lossy' and 'lossless'

Standard file formats	Properties	Limitations
JPEG (.jpg) (Joint Photographic Expert Group)	• Lossy raster image file • Compression rate can be adjusted to compress a lot or not as much • Can be used for print and digital work	• Quality is lost over time and through use
TIFF (.tif) (Tagged Image File Format)	• A flexible raster image format • Lossless, uncompressed raster file • Retains layers in a similar way to native file types or can be saved as a flattened (no layers) version • High quality and good depth of colour • Can make parts of it transparent • Useful for representing scanned documents	• Large file size – all but the smallest files are too large to send by email or use on websites • Can take a long time to open and download • Not all programmes can open TIFF files
BMP (.bmp) (Bitmap)	• Uncompressed • Very high quality • Supports various colour palettes and depths • Colour data is stored for every single pixel	• Very large file size • Does not scale up very well
PNG (.png) (Portable Graphics Format)	• Lossless compression • Designed for images on the internet • Good for images with blocks of colour • Can handle millions of colours • Can make parts of it transparent	• Some internet browsers do not support it • File is still large after compression • Only supports RGB (Red Green Blue) colour mode, which is intended for screen displays rather than CMYK (Cyan, Magenta, Yellow, Key – also known as black) which is intended for print

Table 1.36: Continued

Standard file formats	Properties	Limitations
GIF (.gif) (Graphics Interchange Format)	• Lossless compression • Small file size • Accessible for all internet browsers • Can make parts of it transparent • Can apply simple animation to it • Limited to a palette of 256 colours	• Reduces number of colours in the image when being compressed • Images can look washed out • Most GIFs are very small in dimensions • Image quality often quite poor
EPS (.eps) (Encapsulated PostScript)	• Vector file type • Good for illustrations and vector artwork • Very high quality for print • An older file type	• Cannot be easily opened without specialist software such as Photoshop • Does not allow **transparency**
PDF (.pdf) (Portable Document Format)	• Can be used in conjunction with Photoshop to maintain layers • Reproduces text well • Very accessible file type that can be opened easily using free software • Can be easily created from word processed documents • Compressible • Customisable to stop editing or printing • Can be interactive	• Once a PDF has been created, unless it still has its layers, it is not easily editable • Although free to view, it is not usually free to edit as it needs specialist software

Static image file formats

As the name suggests, static image files are suitable for storing digital images. These images could be raster images or vector graphics.

Raster images

Raster images are digital scans, photographs, artworks or illustrations that are composed of tiny individual squares called pixels. Raster images are a type of Bitmap (.bmp) image file, which is a large file that saves all its colour data without compressing any of it. See Topic Area 2 in Unit R094, 'file compression'.

Figure 1.49: Usually, pixelation like this is not a good thing. When might such pixelation be needed?

When you see an image on TV that has been blurred out, this is called 'pixelation'. It happens because that portion of the raster image has been enlarged so that the individual, coloured blocks or pixels become visible, when usually we would not be able to spot them.

Vector graphics

Vector graphics are digital line diagrams or graphics with block colours and shapes that can be scaled up or down to any resolution without becoming distorted because they are not made up of pixels.

Vector graphics are made out of paths, which are basically mathematical equations that become points on the screen, connected by lines and curves.

Figure 1.50: Why do you think vector graphics have such an impact when added to a media product?

Audio files

Audio files store digital sound only. Like with image file formats, you can change their file size using both lossy and lossless compression. See Unit R094, Topic Area 2, 'Compression settings' to see how file compression works. You can also edit, layer and arrange individual sound files to create audio media products.

The properties of digital audio files

The properties of digital audio files that affect the quality of the sound we hear are the **sample rate** and **bit depth**.

Sample rate

Digital sound waves are broken down into thousands of pieces of data called samples. The sample rate is the number of these pieces of data that have been captured per second. The more samples that are taken, the more detail there is in the sound waves. The more detail there is, the better the sound quality.

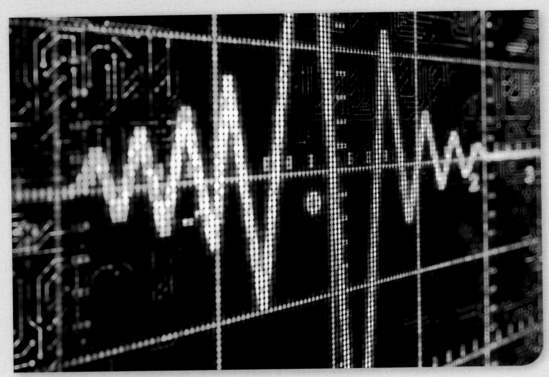

Figure 1.51: Why do you think it is so important to be able to see sound waves visually?

Each sample represents a measurement called **amplitude**. The amplitude measurement is the height of a sound wave from the middle of the wave to its highest or lowest point. The sample rate is measured in hertz (Hz). The most common audio sample rate is 44 100 Hz.

A higher audio sample rate will maximise sound quality, but the file size will be larger.

Bit depth

Bit depth is the number of units of data available for each sound clip. Each unit is called a **bit**. The higher the number of bits, the higher the quality of the audio file and the less likely the sound will distort when played loud. A CD will usually have a bit depth of 16 bits.

Audio file formats

There are many different audio file formats that are used for different scenarios. Some of these audio file formats use lossy compression and others use lossless compression. See 'file compression' in Unit R094, Topic Area 2 to remind yourself about the difference between lossy and lossless compression.

The more common audio file formats are outlined in Table 1.37.

Table 1.37: Common audio file formats

Audio file format	Compression	Why choose this file format?	Limitations
MP3 (.mp3) (MPEG-1 Audio Layer 3)	Compressed (lossy)	• Works on most devices (standard) • Very small file	• Fine for export to the consumer, but not high enough quality for professional recording • Can sound tinny, muddy or have hissing noises
AAC (.aac) (Advanced Audio Coding)	Compressed (lossy)	• Very small file • Good for streaming, especially on mobile phones • Better sound quality than MP3 • Standard sound file for Apple devices	• Not compatible with all devices/platforms • Still loses some quality
Ogg Vorbis (.ogg)	Compressed (lossy)	• Used by Spotify • More efficient and better quality than MP3	• Compression results in some loss of data
FLAC (.flac) (Free Lossless Audio Codec)	Compressed (lossless)	• Free • Used by Tidal • Studio quality sound • Compresses to nearly half the size of uncompressed files without losing quality	• File sizes are up to six times larger than MP3 • Not supported by some streaming apps such as iTunes
ALAC (.m4a) (Apple Lossless Audio Codec)	Compressed (lossless)	• Supported by iTunes • Safely converts to other formats without losing quality	• Compression is not quite as efficient as FLAC • Large file sizes • Really only compatible with Apple devices
WAV (.wav) (Waveform Audio)	Uncompressed	• High-quality sound • CDs are encoded as WAV files • Identical copy of the original music	• Huge file sizes
AIFF (.aiff) (Audio Interchange File Format)	Uncompressed	• Apple alternative to WAV • Highly compatible with GarageBand, Logic Pro and Apple Loops software • Identical copy of the original music	• Big file sizes

How you choose an audio file format depends on several factors. Firstly, it depends on what equipment you are using and whether it will only use specific native file formats. If you do not have an Apple computer then some file types will not be available to you, and vice versa.

Secondly, it depends on the purpose of your audio recording. If you are recording an interview for a podcast, for example, you would potentially choose a WAV file. If you are then uploading it to the internet and sharing it, you may decide to export it to an MP3 as this will have a much smaller file size, that will load much more quickly.

Soundscapes for films are generally made up of layers of different digital and live sounds, most of which are created in a studio. To achieve the sound quality needed to match up with the picture quality, you may need to use a WAV or FLAC file format. Many broadcast stations, professional TV and audio-visual studios use an extension of the WAV file called the BWF (Broadcasting Wave Format). If you would just like to add a short sound or audio clip to a much bigger product such as a multimedia kiosk product then an MP3 may well be all that you need.

Figure 1.52: What do you think the computer screen will look like as more layers of sound are added?

Moving image files

Moving image files are also called video files and they are in fact a collection of images, audio and other data. They are a lot more complex than audio files or still image files. Moving image files include DVDs, streamed programmes, social media videos and live footage.

There are many ways to encode and save moving image data, but the use of different file formats does not necessarily relate to the quality of the video within them. For example, one file format is a MOV file – this could contain a low-quality video for a pop-up on a website, or it could contain HD quality footage from three cameras layered with extra sound and special effects. You cannot know from the file format what kind of video file it is, unless you look at the size of the file or open it.

The properties of digital moving image file formats

Moving images are not actually moving at all. Video is in fact made up of a series of still images, viewed in an order that makes sense when played at a certain speed. This gives the idea of action and motion. Each of these still images is called a frame.

Every video file has properties that make up the video signal being stored. Two important properties that affect the quality of a video product are **frame rate** and resolution. Aspect ratio is another important property which is also covered to explain resolution.

Frame rate

The frame rate is how quickly images in a video file are shown. So, if in a single second the audience is shown 30 frames, then the frame rate is 30 frames per second (fps). When you show an audience so many frames so quickly, the human eye cannot detect each individual frame, so our brains are tricked into thinking that they are seeing one smooth motion.

Frame rate can have an impact on the style of the film as well as the way that the audience views it. If you changed the frame rate in a section of a video you can slow the action down (slow motion), or speed it up so that the action becomes blurred.

The frame rate needed depends on both the content and the type of video product being filmed. Examples:

- Most mainstream films are usually shown at 24 fps because this frame rate is most like real life.

- Live concerts and sporting events may use higher frame rates (approximately 30 fps) because there is a lot of speed and action. By capturing more frames, the motions will still appear smooth, and details will not be lost.

- A video game might need a higher frame rate (between 30 fps and 60 fps), particularly if there is a lot of movement in the frame from different areas on the screen. Detail enhances the gameplay and players can see all the elements in the game that they need to interact with.

Figure 1.53: How many frames do you think might be recorded for a full-length feature film?

Let's get creative!

Have you ever made a flip book? If so, you were using the same concept as frames in a video.

1 Create your own flip book with 24 frames in it.

- Choose a simple idea to represent, such as a frog jumping off a lily pad, or a person running across the page.

- Draw your frames on a small, thick stack of paper starting from the back and working forward so that you can see the previous drawing through the page.

- Each frame should be slightly different to the one behind it to create the illusion of movement.

Continued

- Staple down the left-hand side for a book spine.

- Now, flip through the pages as quickly as you can, hold your thumb on the bottom right-hand edge and let each page go, one after the other. See if you can get through 24 frames in a second.

2 What would be the effect if you put even more frames in?

Aspect ratio

Aspect ratio is the dimensions for displaying a video or image – usually a video will be wider than it is high. For example, a video that has a 1:1 aspect ratio would have a height the same size as the width, so it would be a square.

A 16:10 aspect ratio, which is a common ratio for computer screens and tablets, would mean that the width of the display, whatever size it is, would always be 1.6 times the height.

Resolution (SD, HD, UHD, 4K, 8K)

Just as with static image file formats, moving image resolution refers to the number of pixels in each frame. Instead of using pixels per inch (PPI) to determine resolution, resolution is based on the aspect ratio of the video.

Resolution is measured by the number of pixels that can be included in a particular aspect ratio, such as a ratio of 16:9, which is the most common ratio for television screens. A high number of pixels would mean a higher resolution and therefore higher-quality video. A smaller number of pixels would lead to a lower-resolution video. Outlined below are the main screen resolution types:

- **Standard definition (SD):** Any resolution that is under 720 pixels is called Standard Definition (SD). Fewer and fewer video projects are being shot in SD because the screens that they are being shown on are so good and the video will lack depth and detail.

- **High definition (HD):** 720 pixels and over, up to 1080 pixels is considered High Definition (HD). Many videos are shot in HD, particularly video for web and some television shows.

- **Full HD:** 1080 or more pixels is called full HD and has become the industry standard for the filming of most mainstream films and high-quality television programmes. The footage appears crisp and detailed, but the video files do not take up too much storage. It is also a popular screen resolution for smartphones.

- **4K or Ultra HD (UHD):** 3800 pixels or more is known as 4K or Ultra HD. Intense colours and in-depth zooms come across well when filmed in Ultra HD. This is useful for filmmakers but matters less to the audience.

- **8K:** 7600 pixels or more is known as 8K, but this is very rarely used to shoot films. This is extremely high resolution, and it can be useful for green screens or zooming very long distances without losing definition.

As with computer monitors, it doesn't matter what resolution a film has been shot in – if the screen it is being viewed on does not support that resolution, then the extra definition and detail will not be seen.

For example, the world's first 8K television was created by Sharp in 2012, but it has taken until 2021 for them to be mass produced. Costing over £1500 in 2021, most 8K televisions will also need streaming over a 5G internet connection with high-speed cables so that the huge amounts of pixel data can come through quickly enough.

Figure 1.54: What do you think will be the next format after 8K?

Moving image file formats

As with static image and audio file formats, there are many different options to choose from. There is no one size fits all when it comes to file formats; it is down to the technical team to work out what file format is best for the product based on its purpose, context and audience.

The common moving image file formats are outlined in Table 1.38. See Unit R094, Topic Area 2, 'Compression settings' to see how file compression works.

Table 1.38: Common moving image file formats

File format	Moving image type	Compression	Properties	Limitations
MP4	Video, animation	Compressed (lossy)	• Used on multiple platforms and operating systems • Small file sizes • Standard on the web	• Audio and video can go out of sync • Loss of quality if compressed too much
MOV	Video, animation	Compressed (lossy)	• QuickTime file developed by Apple • Used for editing more than playback	• Not many devices have QuickTime
WMV	Video, animation	Compressed (lossy)	• Streaming is possible directly from this file type • Good video quality • High compression	• Only available on Windows without downloading a player • Not commonly used
AVI (Audio Video Interleaved)	Video, animation	• Compressed (lossy) • Uncompressed (lossless)	• Choice of compressed or uncompressed files • Good quality	• No direct streaming is possible • Menus and chapters are not supported
ANIMATED GIF	Animation	Compressed (lossless)	• Easy to make • Small file sizes • Can be viewed on any device • Compresses without losing much quality • Supported by web browsers	• For short videos only • Once finished cannot be edited again • Images can look blocky because the colour depth is low

Filmmakers spend large amounts of time and energy making adverts, video game scenes, films, TV programmes and music videos. Even tiny GIFs and looped clips that are a small part of much larger websites and multimedia products take time to produce. These efforts would go to waste if the moving image footage they produce is not saved and distributed in the most suitable file type.

For example, a high-end, full HD-quality film is unlikely to have the impact that the director was hoping for if it is distributed using highly compressed MP4 files. Instead an AVI or a WMV file may be more appropriate for this kind of moving image file. However, a short, funny, banner advert on a social media page would need to be of a small and highly compatible file size, so a MOV or AVI file would not be suitable, while an MP4 or maybe a GIF file would be.

Review your learning

Test your knowledge

1 Name three factors that a film company will need to take into consideration when distributing a feature film.

2 Explain which file type would be best for distribution of the following media products:

a   a TV advert

b   a magazine

c   a radio programme

d   a short-looped video on a website.

3 Why might creators of a media product choose several different platforms for their media product?

What have you learnt?

	See section
• Distribution platforms and media to reach audiences.	4.1
• Properties and formats of media files.	4.2

Visual identity and digital graphics

Let's get started

Why do you think businesses use colours in their branding? Do you think a brand would be as recognisable if it used different colours?

What will you learn in this unit?

Any successful brand for a business, product or service will have a clear and engaging visual identity that communicates its values to existing and potential consumers. There are a variety of components that make up visual identity, including logos, shapes, fonts, colours and the layout of a graphic. By understanding these features, you will be able to plan and create your own digital graphic for an intended target audience.

In this unit you will learn about:

- visual identity **TA1**
- digital graphics for products **TA2**
- visual identity and digital graphics **TA3**.

How you will be assessed

This unit will be assessed through a series of coursework tasks that show your understanding of each topic area. You will complete the tasks independently in class with teacher supervision. The assignment will be marked by your teacher. The assignment contains two tasks, which will cover:

- planning a visual identity for a digital graphic product
- creating the visual identity and graphic product.

Develop visual identity

Let's get started

Look at the figure below. If each image was a **logo** for a different business, what do you think each business would sell or promote?

Figure 2.1: Do you think these logos are effective even though they are only in black and white?

What will you learn?

- Purpose, elements and design of visual identity.

1.1 Purpose, elements and design of visual identity

In this section you will look at how **visual identity** is created and used by businesses. You will also look into how the visual identity of a brand creates an impression of their products or services on audiences.

What is meant by visual identity?

Visual identity consists of any graphical or image-based content used by a brand. This visual content may be a logo, a shop front or even what is on a carrier bag. It is used to create an impression on consumers, which enables them to understand what products and/or services are offered by the brand.

Why is visual identity important?

Businesses use their visual identity to tell consumers about their brands without having to rely on words alone. Visual identity helps to establish the brand of a business, product or service. It enables businesses to make more sales because consumers return to buy the products or services again and again. A business or product/service brand with a strong visual identity can communicate well with their target audiences.

Familiarity and brand loyalty

The visual identity of a brand should be recognisable to consumers. It enables them to easily find or recall the brand's products and/ or services. The parts of a visual identity that make a brand recognisable include the brand's name and also the colours, logos and typography used. When a brand becomes familiar, audiences may refer to the brand rather than the product they sell – for example, people asking for the brand name 'Sellotape' rather than the product sticky tape.

Once a brand is familiar to audiences, the products and/or services it offers also become easily recognisable to customers. For example, while Coca-Cola is the brand, the many products it offers are easily identifiable to customers, because they all have a similar visual identity. This is sometimes referred to as **establishing a brand**.

It is important to understand that the **brand identity** of a business is different from that of the visual identity of a product and/or service.

Business brand

A business brand will have a visual style that is unique, to help separate it from other brands. Google or Yahoo are examples of business brands.

Product or service brand

A product or service brand may use the same or a similar visual identity to the business brand. For example, Google Books, Google News and Google Maps each have their own visual identity, which separates them from each other but which still identifies them all as part of the business brand Google.

However, it is not always the case that product or service brands have the same or a similar visual identity to their related business brand. Some products or services have a completely different visual identity to the business brand of which they are a part. For example, Walkers crisp products each have a different visual identity, yet they are all recognisable as Walkers branded crisps because they share the Walkers logo.

Figure 2.2: What do the crisp packages in this picture have in common?

Brand loyalty

Over time consumers may develop either business brand or product/service **brand loyalty**. Brand loyalty is where consumers prefer to spend money with a particular brand because they trust it or are more familiar with it than they are with others. Product/service brand loyalty is where consumers purchase or use products/services that they have used previously and found useful or enjoyed.

Figure 2.3: Why would brands with high customer loyalty be more successful in the long term?

Visual identity is important for brand loyalty as it helps customers remain loyal to them. Some brands such as John Lewis and Nike have kept their branding and visual identity consistent throughout many years. Often, only slight changes are made to the colours, **fonts** and graphics so that customers can easily recognise the brand.

> **Over to you!**   1
>
> Find out about three different business brands that you know by doing some desk research. Record how the brands have changed over time and make sure you focus on the colours, fonts and any graphic(s) that may have been altered as the brands have evolved over time.

Visual communication

Visual identity is used to communicate to consumers the nature of a business and their products/services. Businesses communicate visual identity to consumers by using different types of graphics. Using visual graphics is one of the most effective methods of getting a consumer's attention. Visual communication includes advertising media such as posters, leaflets, magazine covers, billboards and web adverts.

Using visual communication helps to promote long-term memories, which helps further embed a brand with a consumer. It also helps consumers to digest information because it is often easier to understand an image than a page full of text. Imagine you are on holiday in France and want an ice cream. If you saw a picture of an ice cream in a café window you would be confident that they would sell them. Otherwise, you would have to know the word for 'ice cream' in French and look for it on a menu.

Visual communication also involves graphics such as infographics, flow charts, mind maps and presentations. These forms of communication have to rely heavily on imagery to help the consumer understand their content. By using graphics, shapes and images a business can easily deliver the message they want to communicate. Different situations will need information to be presented using different forms of visual communication. For example, a business presentation will use graphics alongside text to help the audience understand what is being communicated, whereas in a report there may be more text with the only visual element being charts or graphs.

Figure 2.4: Why are billboards so effective at delivering messages to audiences?

Component features of visual identity

As mentioned previously there are different components that make up a business or product/service brand's visual identity. The component features of visual identity include the name of the business or the product/services it offers, its logo and the slogan/strap line that the brand may have. Most brands will have all three components of visual identity, even if they are not all well-known. For example, a business or the products/services it offers may have a very memorable name and logo, but not everyone may be aware of its slogan.

Brand identity

Visual identity is closely linked to brand identity, but it is important to understand that they are two different concepts. While visual identity is all the visual elements of a brand, brand identity also includes non-visual elements. Non-visual elements of brand identity include the values or principles of a brand, and how the brand is unique when compared to the competition.

A good visual identity will also capture the brand identity of a brand (business or product/service). The brand identity is often tied in with elements of the visual identity such as the graphics or colours used in the visual identity. For example, a health food shop may choose to use the colour green in its visual identity because this represents its brand identity of being about nature.

If the visual identity and brand identity of a business or product/service brand match, the brand will flourish because consumers will know exactly what it stands for. They will feel confident in purchasing or using that brand. If the visual and brand identities do not match up, consumers may feel confused at the message the brand is trying to get across. This will have a negative impact because consumers may be put off the brand and so will not purchase its products or use its services.

Name

The name of a business or the products/services it offers is possibly the most important element in helping the audience remember it. The name is what consumers will look for when looking for a product on a shelf and when they discuss the product the name is what they will mention to others. The visual design of the brand's name is equally important and a variety of factors must be taken into consideration such as font, colour(s) and size. Some brands have very distinct brand names that stand out from the crowd.

Figure 2.5: Why do you think chocolate bars are named as they are?

Table 2.1 further illustrates this using some key business types.

Table 2.1: Business and product/service brand name categories

Type	Description	Examples
Descriptive	Names that describe or tell the consumer what the business, products or services are about	Burger King (business) or the Big Whopper (product) Poundland (business) iPlayer (service)
Acronym	These are businesses, products or services that use the first letter of each word to make up the brand name	EA: Electronic Arts (business) BBC: British Broadcasting Association (business)
Founder	The name of the person(s) who thought of or developed the business or product/service over time is used as the brand name	Adidas, founder Adi Dassler (business) Kellogg's, founder William Keith Kellogg (business)
Real words	These businesses, products or services use words for their brand names that are the same or similar to descriptions of what the business makes or does	Twitter (business and service) Photoshop (product) Nike Air Force 1 trainers (product)

Logo

The logo of a business or product/service brand can be just as important as the name. For a logo to stand out it needs to be unique. The visual design of a logo is made up of different factors such as colours, graphics, shapes and text. A logo that works well will usually be quite simple in its design.

Brand logos can be grouped into different styles, as shown in Table 2.2.

Table 2.2: Brand logo styles

Style	Definition	Examples
Picture	An image or graphic is used to represent the brand	Apple Twitter
Emblem	Often looks like a badge; it can include the name of the brand too	UPS Warner Brothers
Character	If a brand has a signature character they might decide to use this as part of their logo	KFC: Colonel Sanders Haribo: Bear Frosties: Tony the Tiger
Letterform	A single letter stylised to fit the visual identity of a brand or business	Netflix Honda
Abstract	Sometimes the most difficult style of logo to get right, this style uses shapes and colours but will not have an immediate or clear link to the purpose of the business or product/service	Spotify Pepsi

Each logo style has advantages and disadvantages. However, choosing the right logo is incredibly important to the success of a brand. If a business later realise that a logo does not quite look right or represent the business or product/service correctly, they will have to make a decision. Either:

- change the logo and potentially confuse consumers who are loyal to their business or product/service brand, or

- keep the logo, but new consumers may not associate the logo with the business or product/service type.

Figure 2.6: Where do you think these logos might be used in the real world?

Over to you!   2

Find three logos for each of the following types of business sector by doing some desk research.

- Cars
- Entertainment (Films or games developers)
- Shops

Answer these questions about the brand logos you have researched.

1   Identify the similarities and differences between the logos within each sector.

2   Explain why each type of business would have different styles of logo.

3   Decide which logo works best for each business sector and why.

Slogan or strap line

The **slogan** or strap line of a brand is something that consumers remember. Slogans or strap lines will often include key words that are important to the brand or words that the business (or product/service) want to be associated with. Usually, a slogan or strap line makes use of a linguistic device such as a **catchphrase**, a **metaphor** or even **alliteration**. These linguistic devices help the slogan stick in the consumer's head and makes it become familiar.

Figure 2.7: Can you think of any slogans/strap lines for other supermarkets? What makes them memorable?

Slogans/strap lines also need to be short and concise, usually only a few words long. Otherwise, audiences will get bored of reading them. Audiences may potentially see hundreds of adverts per day via posters, the internet and TV, so having a short and effective slogan can help a brand stand out to their potential consumers. Businesses need to be very wary about changing the slogan/strap line of an established brand (business or product/service). Changing an established slogan/strap line can easily cause confusion for consumers and potentially change the impression that the brand gives off to new audiences.

Over to you!   3

Research different slogans from a variety of business and product/service brands. Identify at least one of each of the following.

- A slogan that has a catchphrase

- A slogan that uses a metaphor

- A slogan that uses alliteration

Once you have found an example for each type of slogan, justify which type you think is most effective and why.

Elements of visual identity

A name, logo and slogan can all be considered to be the components of visual identity. In this section you will look at the different elements that make up these components of visual identity. You will learn how these elements can have an impact on consumers' perceptions of a brand.

It is also important to remember that there are many aspects that impact on a brand's visual identity such as business type, brand values and brand positioning in terms of price. These aspects will be look at in more detail later in this topic area.

Graphics

Graphics are any images, shapes or symbols used in a brand's visual identity. They represent or enhance the message that the product is trying to convey to the audience/consumer. These graphics can be created through drawing, either on a computer or by hand. Alternatively, they can be more complex and sometimes involve many different graphics that are put together to make a final detailed graphic. The style of a graphic will depend on the purpose of the graphic and the context that it is to be used in.

Sometimes the graphics used by a business or product/service brand may be abstract. This means that they may be made up of a combination of shapes that do not actually represent anything. Alternatively, a brand may use a graphic that represents the product or service it is trying to promote. For example, if the product was an energy drink, the graphic used might try to incorporate a drinks bottle into the visual design in some way.

This may be included as part of their logo or the brand name could be shaped so it looks like a bottle. Using a graphic in this way would instantly let consumers know that the product is a drink or bottle, before they even read the brand name.

Figure 2.8: Which sectors do you think these graphics could be used for and why?

Graphics are not just used as logos. Think about Apple devices such the iPhone or iPad, where each of the graphics on the operating system makes up part of Apple's visual identity. The phone icon, the message icon and the email icon will have all been designed to fit in with the brand's visual identity. Each graphic a business uses in their branding will usually be scrutinised and debated over by a team of creative media professionals in that business. This is because if the graphics are done well, they may be used by that brand for years to come.

With some product/service brands this approach is taken a step further. For example, the Samsung Galaxy brand of phone handsets may all look visually different in their styling, but the operating system is the same on all of them.

Figure 2.9: Why do you think having a consistent set of graphics helps a brand to feel familiar to audiences?

Several technology brands follow this format, as it means when consumers upgrade to a new phone from the same brand they will already be familiar with how to use it.

Typography

Not only are the words important for a brand's image but the way a brand's name and slogan are displayed can have just as big an impact as the words themselves. Effective typography ensures that the text on a piece of branding is easy to read, clear and appeals to the consumer. Using typography that relates to a brand will help it in the following ways.

- It helps an audience to recognise the business or product/service more easily as they associate the brand with the typography.

- It gains the attention of the audience, allowing them to appreciate what is being promoted.

- It encourages decision-making from an audience as if the typography is effective, it will help to reinforce the brand's message.

- It creates an emotional response from an audience – for example, if a product has used a similar-style typography for many years the audience may be emotionally taken back to when they first used the product.

Figure 2.10, on the next page, shows the main features of typography. To learn more about how typography is used in graphic design, see 'Typography' in Topic Area 2.

Let's get creative!   1

Think of a business that you would like to create the visual identity for (either a real business or one you have made up). This business might be one that sells products used for a hobby, or a creative or sporting activity.

Design a typeface, including three different font styles, that is suitable for this business. Give reasons for your choices.

Serif and sans serif

Serif and sans serif are two types of lettering. Each lettering style gives a different impression to audiences.

Serif letters have flicks or strokes attached to the end of the letter shapes, e.g. Georgia. They are best used for printed media. These lettering styles would usually be thought of as traditional and elegant. They are often used by professional businesses.

Sans serif letters do not have these decorative flicks, e.g. Arial. They are best used for digital media or on websites. These lettering styles are associated with brands which are modern and embrace simplicity. Technology brands often use sans serif fonts.

Typefaces and fonts

Typefaces are families of lettering styles known as fonts. They are grouped into families because they are similar in appearance, e.g. Arial or Georgia.

A font refers to the weight, width and style of the typeface. Fonts in the Arial family: **Arial Black**, Arial Narrow, Arial Nova. Fonts in the Georgia family: **Georgia Bold**, Georgia Regular. A brand may aim to use one or two font styles and one typeface. If too many typefaces are used this can cause the visual identity of the business or product/service brand to appear confused.

Typography

Hierarchy

There should be a clear hierarchy of importance in the appearance of text. This is usually indicated to audiences using different text sizes. Usually, the more important the text the larger it will be. The brand name of a business or product/service will usually be the largest in size, the slogan will be slightly smaller and any other text will be smaller than the slogan.

Contrast

The level of contrast can help portray the importance of a message. A high level of contrast can indicate that a message or idea is important, while a low level of contrast can indicate that it is not as important.

Consistency

Most designers will only utilise two or three different typefaces or font styles for a particular business or product/service brand to ensure consistency and give the brand a clean visual identity. If too many typefaces are used this can cause the visual identity of the business or product/service brand to appear confused.

Figure 2.10: How can the different features of typography impact on the visual identity of a business or product brand?

Colour palette and meaning

Visual designers of brands have a large **colour palette** to use in their designs. They will usually choose between one and three colours to use for the visual identity of a brand. A good designer will be consistent with their use of colour.

The colours used by a brand will be used alongside the other elements of the visual identity, such as typography and any graphics or shapes. A strong visual identity will successfully combine these elements into a brand that gives a good impression to audiences.

Different colours are associated with different feelings and emotions. They are often used by brands to help shape the perception audiences have and to create an emotional response to the brand, which helps to create brand loyalty. Business and product/service brands use colour to inform consumers of what they want them to think and feel about the brand. For example, a cleaning product brand may choose to use white in their visual identity because this colour is associated with cleanliness.

Table 2.3 shows some of the potential meanings associated with different colours and therefore which brands might use these colours. These associated meanings are also called connotations.

Table 2.3: Colour meanings and their use in visual identities

Colour	Associated meanings (connotations)	Brands that use it
Red	Passion, excitement, love, fire; often associated with playful or modern brands; however, also represents anger or danger	Cola-Cola Nintendo
Green	Can represent a variety of meanings varying from eco-friendliness, wealth to renewal; also nature, good luck, health and sickness, jealousy, life	Greenpeace Starbucks
Blue	Trust and reliability; certain shades are also associated with calmness, rest, peace, patience; freedom or escape	Visa Facebook
Yellow	Friendliness, happiness, creativity, optimism, warmth, cheerfulness; however, in some contexts can also represent sickness, cowardly behaviour or danger/hazards (especially if paired with black)	McDonald's Snapchat
Purple	Usually seen as a colour representing luxury/wealth/indulgence, nobility, royalty, wisdom; can represent peace, independence, magic	Cadbury Yahoo
Orange	Playfulness, energy, warmth, joy, fun, excitement, strength; brands will use it to stand out from others	Fanta SoundCloud

Table 2.3: Continued

Colour	Associated meanings (connotations)	Brands that use it
Black	Elegance, authority, power; however, it also has negative meanings such as mystery, fear, darkness, shadows, evil	Mercedes-Benz Nike
White	Purity, innocence, cleanliness, health, perfection, goodness, heaven, simplicity, safety; white may be used on top of another colour to ensure it stands out	Adidas Apple
Gold/ silver	Purity, wealth, grandeur, courage, wisdom, hope, pride	Rolex Lindt

To help designers find colours that will work well together they may use a colour wheel. A colour wheel has:

- **primary colours** (red, blue and yellow)

- **secondary colours** (green, purple and orange), which are created by mixing certain primary colours

- **tertiary colours**, which are created by mixing certain secondary colours.

By splitting the colour wheel in half, you will have:

- **warm colours** (reds, oranges and yellows), which are associated with energy, warmth and friendliness. These are the colours that are first seen by the audience.

- colours that are left, called **cool colours** (blues, greens and purples). These are associated with calmness and are often regarded more as background colours.

By dividing the colour wheel up in different ways, you can identify colours that work well together. For example, analogous colours are three colours grouped together on the colour wheel. Complementary colours are opposite each other on the colour wheel. Triadic colours are three colours equally spaced around the colour wheel.

Figure 2.11: Can you identify the different colour types in this image?

Layout and complexity

Once a business has decided on the graphics, typography and the colour palette of its visual identity, it needs to combine them. This is not always as easy as it might seem. When putting a visual identity design style together, consideration needs to be given to the sizing of the different elements and their spacing. The fewer features a design has, the simpler it will appear. This can be useful if a business wants to be seen as modern or 'to the point'. A complex visual design may look effective, but if consumers cannot easily identify what the business or product/service is from the design, this would have a negative impact on the success of the brand.

Orientation

The orientation of a design is usually landscape (horizontal) or portrait (vertical). The orientation of a design is important, particularly when graphics are used. The brand's visual identity may be used in a variety of different locations, such as on a website, billboard or on product packaging. For example, a website graphic might be designed to only be viewed in a landscape orientation on a desktop computer or laptop. However, when the same website is viewed on a phone, with a portrait orientation, the graphic may become distorted and lose its impact on the audience. Visual designers can overcome technical problems like this, but they must be briefed to consider both orientations when creating their designs.

Layering

When creating branding, visual designers can create complex images by the layering of images. The result can be very effective and often contain hidden meanings. For example, the Museum of London's logo is actually made up of the rough shape of London during various periods in time and the name of the museum is overlaid on top (see Figure 2.12). This creates a visual design that is striking and has extra hidden meaning.

Figure 2.12: Can you use the internet to find any other logos with hidden meanings?

Alignment

Alignment, placement and symmetry are also important when creating a visual identity design style. A visual designer may choose to align the different elements in the centre, which will create a sense of symmetry and be pleasing on the eye. Alternatively, they may choose to align the elements to the left or right; this may make the content easier to read but may not be as visually appealing.

Placement means the positioning of different elements on a graphic. For example, an icon or symbol could be placed on the top right of a graphic and the logo could be placed on the bottom centre. Table 2.4 shows how the elements in a graphic can be placed.

Table 2.4: Placement grid for elements in a graphic

Top left	Top middle	Top right
Middle left	Middle middle	Middle right
Bottom left	Bottom middle	Bottom right

Symmetry is also important because when graphical elements are balanced and symmetrical the design is easier to see and understand. A disadvantage to symmetrical designs is that they can be considered boring. Asymmetrical design has the opposite effect. It is seen as dynamic and energetic. However, if an asymmetrical design is not done well it could be more difficult to understand.

Combining elements of visual identity

Once the separate elements of visual identity have been decided upon, they need to be combined. This process creates the final visual identity of a business or product/service brand. It is important that the elements work well together because otherwise the visual identity may not create the intended emotional response in the audience.

It is important to remember that different audiences/consumers have different wants and needs. For example, consider IKEA and John Lewis: both are large homeware businesses. While being in the same market (homeware), the visual identity of the two businesses is very different. IKEA's visual identity uses bright colours and cartoon style graphics in their instructions. It also uses a big, bulky typography. This indicates to consumers that their brand is fun and energetic. By comparison, John Lewis' visual identity uses black and white primarily, real-life graphics in their instructions, and a thin and elegant typeface. This communicates to their consumers that the John Lewis brand is elegant and no nonsense.

Case study

McDonald's branding over time

As businesses evolve and grow, they may choose to refresh their branding. McDonald's is a prime example of how a business has kept refreshing their visual identity while still ensuring consumers stay familiar with the brand. McDonald's have tweaked and changed their visual identity over the decades, embracing revised graphics, colour schemes and slogans. However, since the 1970s there has been a constant in their visual identity in the form of the 'golden arches' – the capital 'M' is always present in their branding.

Figure 2.13: What impact would changing its logo have on McDonald's?

Using the golden arches means that even though the overall visual identity of McDonald's has changed, consumers are still able to easily identify the brand.

Continued

McDonald's visual identity now reflects a cleaner and sharper image, which ties into some of the business's core **brand values** – being a modern and progressive business. Their recent visual identity elements take into consideration more modern design principles such as:

- only having a limited colour palette for each item (no more than three colours)
- using a sans serif font to promote that they are a modern company
- using big blocks of colour to entice consumers.

McDonald's have also implemented successful slogans over time, one of the most recent successes being 'I'm Lovin' It'. This slogan was introduced across the world at the same time. This was a first for their branding strategy and it allowed customers worldwide to receive a consistent message, which helped McDonald's get their point across.

Check your understanding

1 Describe how a brand changing their visual identity can help them stay relevant.

2 Explain how a brand can ensure that they look familiar to audiences if their visual identity changes.

3 Evaluate which is the most important component of a brand: colour scheme, logo or slogan/strap line. Give your reasons.

Visual identity design style

It is important for the many different components and elements of a brand's visual identity to come together to form a cohesive style. The business type, brand values and brand positioning also need to be considered to ensure that the visual identity design style works well and promotes the brand in the desired way.

For example, a coffee shop may want to be thought of as a welcoming and warm place to relax. The designer would take these factors and try to incorporate them into the coffee shop's visual identity, using a suitable logo, colour palette, typography and relevant graphics. They would also take into consideration the business type, in this case a coffee shop, alongside the brand values. Let's say, if the coffee shop only used organic products the designer may try and incorporate this into their design by using relevant graphics or a slogan.

Business type

The type of business impacts on the visual identity of a brand and how it is portrayed. A start-up business may try to have a very original visual identity design style to help set it apart from other businesses that are otherwise the same. If done well, this design will help set them apart from the competition by giving the impression to potential consumers that they have something unique to offer. If not done well, however, the design might put off consumers who could end up being unsure what their business is about.

As seen in Figure 2.14, on the next page, there is a lot of variation in what businesses can sell or offer to consumers. In this way, the business type can have a big impact on the visual identity that is created for the brand. For example, a toy shop would want to give the impression of being friendly and inviting to children. The colours used should be bright and bold to grab attention and the typography should be easy to read. A graphic of a cuddly bear or building blocks might be used to ensure that consumers would associate it with toys.

Let's get creative!　　2

Choose a type of business from Figure 2.14 and create a mood board (TA2, Section 2.3) for its visual identity. Use examples from real-life businesses. For your chosen business type, you should create:

- a colour palette
- a collection of typography styles: the typeface(s) and font styles
- relevant graphics or images.

Brand values

Brand values are principles or aspects that brands want to be associated with. The values of a business or product/service brand may change over time as the brand evolves and grows bigger. The brand values will help shape its identity in terms of what it stands for. This also has an impact on the visual identity of the brand. For example, a food shop may have a focus on recycling and not using single-use plastics. Recycling would be a brand value for the shop and would help influence the visual identity of the brand. In this instance, the food shop might want to ensure that the colours and graphics used in their brand's visual identity promote recycling.

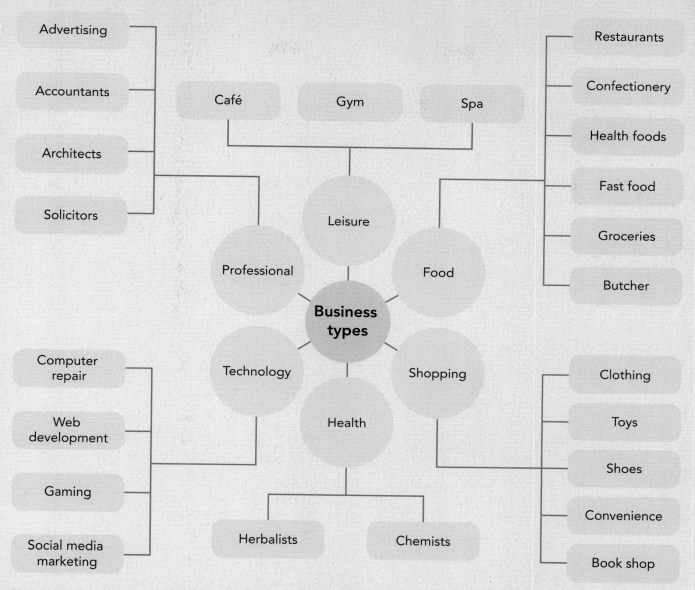

Figure 2.14: How do you think the business type will influence the visual identity elements used in its branding?

There are some values that are more difficult to represent or communicate through a brand's visual identity. When this happens designers think about colours that convey these values to consumers. If a business wants to be seen as responsible, for example, they may have the colour blue in their logo because this colour represents trust. If a business wants to be seen as innovative, they might have a logo that is unique and shows something that has not been done before.

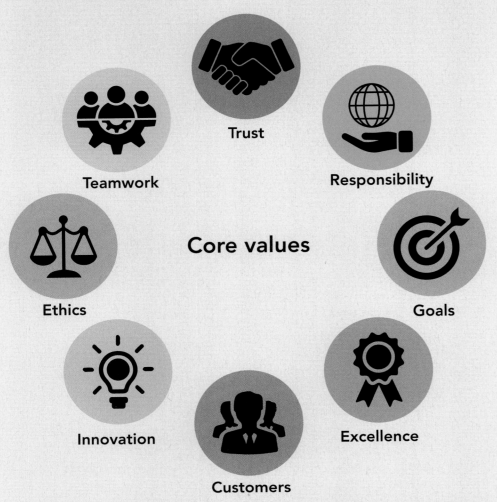

Core values

Teamwork

Trust

Responsibility

Ethics

Goals

Innovation

Customers

Excellence

Figure 2.15: Can you think of other core values that a business may wish to adopt as brand values?

Stretch

The visual identity of a bank is very important. It needs to communicate to consumers that the bank is trustworthy and a safe place to store their consumers' money. Trustworthiness and safety are key brand values for a bank. Complete the following tasks about visual identity and brand values.

1   What other brand values might a bank want to ensure they portray through brand identity?

2   Research a bank and its brand values. Describe how its logo and slogan might help communicate the bank's brand values to consumers.

3   Now think about businesses more generally. Explain how the type of a business, its brand values, and the application of the different component features of visual identity all need to work together for a visual identity to be effective.

Brand positioning

The price of a product or service is important as it is a key factor in how consumers perceive the brand. Most brands will fall into one of three categories: economy, mid-range or high-end. The category that the brand falls into impacts the visual identity it creates.

It is important that brands follow a visual identity design style in keeping with their **brand positioning**, because otherwise it might make it difficult for their **target audience** to identify with them. This is taken into consideration when designing the visual identity of a business or product/service. The audience of a cheaper brand will have different expectations about visual identity from that of a more expensive brand.

It is also important to remember that the same business may have differently positioned products or services to cater to all budgets. This means that the same business might have multiple different brands, each of which is positioned differently in the market. For example, Volkswagen has both economy and mid-range products to appeal to as much of the car market as possible.

Economy brands

Economy brands are lower priced and may be thought of as lower quality than others; however, this is not always true. Many brands are lower priced but can still be as good quality as more expensive alternatives.

Budget or supermarket own-branded products often use bright colours to help attract consumers' attention, alongside lots of images or graphics. These visual identity elements help keep the audience's attention and highlight the low cost of the products or services.

An alternative method some economy brands use to trick their consumers into thinking their products are high quality is to mimic the look of mid-range or even high-end brands. This can have the effect that consumers feel they are buying products that are more luxurious than they really are.

Mid-range brands

Mid-range brands often try to strike a balance between ensuring their visual identity design style looks professional and ensuring they do not put off potential consumers by looking too exclusive, like high-end brands.

They want to show that they are selling a quality product/service but at an affordable price. To achieve this their design style might include elements from both economy and high-end brands. For example, they may use a bright colour palette to attract consumers but graphics that are simple in their nature.

High-end brands

High-end brands are generally the most expensive and perceived as high quality. Many high-end brands are also thought of as luxurious. High-end brands will often choose simplicity in their visual identity, often using a very limited colour palette, such as black and white.

It is thought that high-end brands have to come from established businesses who have operated for many years but this is not always the case. There are many high-end brands that are quite new, offering high-quality products and services.

High-end brands are also seen as niche and tailored to suit a small target audience. This helps promote the idea that high-end brands are exclusive.

In terms of their visual identity, high-end brand visual identities may focus on a single product or service and include slick and sophisticated slogans or strap lines alongside a logo and brand name.

Figure 2.16: What high-end brands and products can you name?

Table 2.5 summarises the differences between economy, mid-range and high-end brand positions.

Table 2.5: Summary of brand positioning

Brand position	Colour palette	Typography	Layout	Examples
Economy	Bright and bold; potentially primary colours	May imitate mid-range or high-end brands	May have a lot of visual features	Aldi, Primark and own-brand products from shops
Mid-range	Up to three colours that complement each other well	Unique to the brand and very identifiable	Will have a logical layout inviting the audience to read/look through	Marks and Spencer, Adidas and Heinz Tomato Ketchup
High-end	Very limited palette, only one or two colours; possibly black and white	Elegant or instantly recognisable	Few visual features but all relevant	Apple, John Lewis and couture fashion

Review your learning

Test your knowledge

1. Identify the different component features of visual identity.

2. Explain why certain business types would have certain colours or features in their visual identity.

3. Explain the difference between visual identity and brand identity.

4. Explain what brand positioning is.

What have you learnt?

	See section
• Purpose, elements and design of visual identity.	1.1

Plan digital graphics for products

Let's get started

Why would a graphic designer want to use a mind map when creating a visual identity for a brand?

What will you learn?

- Graphic design and conventions.
- Properties of digital graphics and use of **assets**.
- Techniques to plan visual identity and digital graphics.

2.1 Graphic design and conventions

In this section you will look at several graphic design concepts and **layout conventions** for different graphic products and purposes.

Concepts of graphic design

The designer of a media product needs to ensure that the visual identity of a business or product brand is applied consistently using several graphic design concepts. These concepts of graphic design include alignment, typography, use of colour and **colour systems** and use of white space.

Application of visual identity

When creating graphic designs for a business or product brand, the designer needs to ensure that the visual identity and house style of the business or product matches. A business or product brand's house style is their preferred design choices and can include:

- fonts that are used on any digital graphics that are created

Figure 2.17: What elements of house style can you identify from this digital graphic?

- colours that represent their business or brand
- the layout of digital graphics on a given graphical product.

Once the visual identity and house style have been decided, graphics can be created. The graphics may be used on the materials that the business or brand creates such as their website, advertisements (both print and digital) and their logo. The graphics created need to incorporate both visual identity and house style so the different **graphical elements** work properly together.

Alignment

How graphical elements are placed on a digital graphic is very important. Different products have different requirements and while alignment may not be something that someone viewing a digital graphic would instantly comment on, it is still a very important part of designing digital graphics. Alignment in graphic design refers to how different assets are lined up. This can be done in a variety of different ways.

Horizontal and vertical alignment

Both horizontal and vertical alignment have the same principle: the **margins** are equal either side of the graphics or content used. It is important to remember that this does not mean that the content is central to the page it is on, but the space the asset occupies. For example, a logo may utilise horizontal alignment even though it is situated in a corner of a completed graphic.

- **Edge alignment:** The graphical elements are aligned to one of the edges (left, right, top or bottom). This type of alignment means all elements will be in line on one side. Edge alignment is usually used in newspapers and web pages as our eyes are familiar with reading content in this way.

- **Centre alignment:** The graphical elements are aligned with the centre of the page or **canvas**. This can be quite difficult to read when there are large amounts of text to be displayed and so is best used when there are a small number of key points to get across. Wedding invites often use this style as it looks very formal.

- **Visual/optical alignment:** Used to help correct errors that may have occurred if another type of alignment is used instead. The graphical elements may not line up but to the eye it is more appealing.

Figure 2.18 shows two different methods of aligning the triangle for the 'play' symbol. Using visual/optical alignment produces a better result.

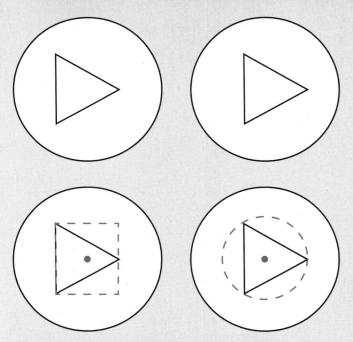

Figure 2.18: Can you think of any other designs where visual or optical alignment are used?

Interrupting alignment

There are also occasions where breaking or interrupting alignment can be used to help punctuate a message to the audience. Breaking alignment creates a focal point on a page where a key message can be placed. This type of alignment should be used sparingly though as too much broken alignment can create a design that is difficult for audiences to read and understand.

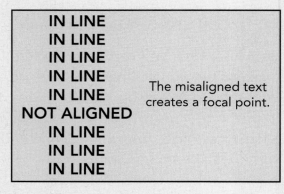

Figure 2.19: Can you think of any other graphics or examples of where breaking alignment has been used to make something stand out?

Over to you!   **1**

Carry out some desk research.

1 Find examples of graphical products (posters, leaflets or websites) that use different types of alignment.

2 Examine the different products and identify the different types of alignment used.

3 How would you have designed the product differently? Explain your reasoning.

Typography

It is very important to remember that typography is used to communicate with consumers. The way letters/words appear can create a feeling, tone, mood or even remind you of a particular brand. The spaces between the letters, weight, size and style of the lettering along with the font type used can make all the difference when making a brand name or logo stand out from the crowd. The style of the font will very much depend on the purpose of the media product as well as who the target audience is. Table 2.6 explains some key typography terms.

Table 2.6: Typography terms. Practise them on a word processing document to help you

Typography term	Explanation	Example
Emphasis	Adding a different style to words or letters to strengthen their impact. Emphasis can come from capitals, boldface, italics, colour. A deeper meaning can be implied by the emphasis used, of importance, contrast or even shouting.	EXAMPLE **Example** *Example*
Font size	The size of a letter or character is measured on a point scale, with each measurement being called a **point**. The larger the point number, the bigger the size of font. Different font families may be different sizes and take up more, or less, space due to the way the fonts have been created. The larger the font, the easier it is to read from a distance, which is particularly useful for adverts on buses and billboards.	10 point 14 point 20 point Arial 12 Times 12
Font type	This is the style of letters or characters that have been designed, also called typeface. These typefaces can be split up into serif and sans serif fonts. Serif fonts have small lines attached to the ends of the larger lines of a letter. Sans serif fonts (sans means 'without' in French) are those letters and characters without the extra lines. A font can create a tone, mood or look when used alongside other design elements. Generally, a large font size is used to gain the attention of an audience. Any other written content will be in a smaller font size. This varies for different graphical products. For example, leaflets may have many headings and sub-headings while a poster has a much smaller number of headings and sub-headings.	**Traditional** Modern DECORATIVE Handwritten STENCIL

An example of effective use of typography is the fashion store Zara's logo, which was redesigned in 2019. The French founder of the design agency that created the logo has also worked for Dior, *Harper's Bazaar* magazine and other high-end, luxury stores, so the new logo seems to fit in with those more expensive designer brands by using a number of similar techniques to inform the audience of its new brand identity. Figure 2.20, on the next page, shows elements of typography working together.

Font type: Typeface is a serif font, so has the extra lines added on the ends. This signifies a brand that has a reputation and history to it, and a classic feel.

Emphasis: Capitalisation of all letters makes a strong statement out of what is simply a name.

Emphasis: Black text on a contrasting, white background helps the text stand out clearly for audiences to see. The use of both black and white helps promote the brand as high end.

Emphasis: The 'A' letters reach up slightly higher than the others, breaking convention of keeping all characters the same height. This creates more impact.

Emphasis: Letters are bold.

Font size: A large font that has taken over a huge proportion of the display window it has been placed on.

Font style: The overlap of the letters suggests that the Zara font does not necessarily conform to the rules that a traditional serif font would suggest.

Figure 2.20: Elements of topography working together in the Zara logo. What would you change about the design?

The font style can help a business or product brand's personality and brand values be communicated to consumers. The business or product brand may choose to use one font style and use the different variants of it such as bold, italic or light. Alternatively, a business or product brand may choose two or three different font styles that complement each other.

Use of colour and colour systems

The use of colour is important with any graphical product and using the right colours is crucial to a business or product brand's visual identity. For example, if a brand or product wants to be thought of as sophisticated they may use white, while a coffee brand may utilise shades of brown to reflect the colour of coffee.

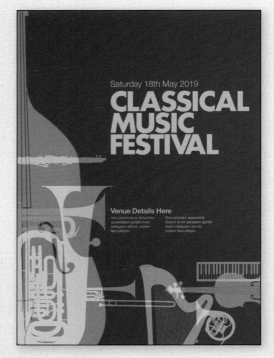

Figure 2.21: How has the designer used a variety of different sized fonts to ensure the poster is easy for audiences to understand?

There are different colour systems for designers to use depending on the type of graphical product that they are creating.

Pantone

The Pantone colour system is based on colour matching and is used to ensure that specific colours can be reproduced regardless of the equipment used. Graphic designers will often use Pantone Colour Systems for graphic design as a base for their work as they will have confidence that their colour choices will be reproduced accurately and it provides an **industry standard**. The Pantone system has over 1000 base colours and there are more colours that are available to match other colour systems.

Each Pantone colour is represented with a unique number. These numbers not only represent the colour but may also have information regarding the material they can be used on. The Pantone Matching System (PMS) would be used for printed items such as packaging or digital content. The Fashion, Home and Interiors system (FHI) would be used for fabrics and textiles, but also cosmetics and paints.

Figure 2.22: What are the benefits of labelling colours with numbers?

Pantone also set trends for others to follow with its 'Colour of the Year'. Since the year 2000 Pantone has selected a colour that takes into consideration the events that have occurred throughout society such as in social media, politics and fashion. Designers may use the colour of the year to tweak business or brand colours to ensure that they stay fresh and current.

Natural Colour System

Like Pantone, the Natural Colour System (NCS) is used to classify colours so designers have an industry standard. The difference between Pantone and NCS is the method by which colours are created. NCS involves the colours white, black, red, yellow, green and blue. NCS is based on the six elementary colours, which are perceived by human beings as being 'pure'. For example, pure green is not perceived to be bluish or yellowish, nor is pure yellow perceived to be greenish or reddish. We can describe all 10 million colours that we can perceive with the six elementary colours (Natural Color System website).

NCS uses two steps to identify and classify colours. First the hue of the colour is found: the mixture of red, yellow, green and blue involved in the colour. The second step is applying the hue to the NCS colour triangle; this has the darkest and lightest version of the hue and everything in between.

NCS identifies colour differently to other colour systems. It defines colours based on their visual appearance and as they are seen by humans. Other systems are based on the practical creating of the colours. It is argued that this allows for colours to be more accurate and correct when humans are experiencing them.

Over to you!   2

Now you know about Pantone and the Natural Colour System:

1   Which one do you think is most useful to designers?

2   In what way does Pantone influence the colours that designers may use?

3   What benefits does the Natural Colour System have when compared to Pantone?

CMYK

The CMYK colour system uses four colours: cyan, magenta, yellow and key (black). This model works by using a white background and masking it with varying amounts of the four colours. It is referred to as a subtractive process as the inks 'subtract' red, green and blue from the white background. As black is also in this colour system, darker blacks can be produced in comparison to other colour systems.

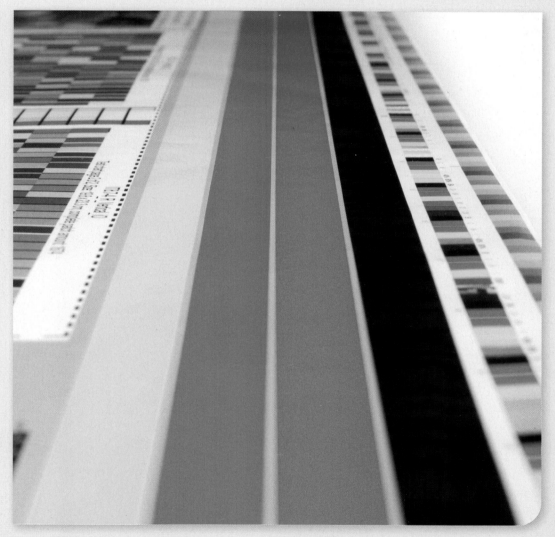

Figure 2.23: Why does CMYK work by adding colours to a white background?

This colour system is the industry standard for print material as it is easier to create additional colours using a white background. Cyan, magenta and yellow are lighter than red, green and blue and when combined these colours can be created.

RGB

RGB uses red, green and blue to create all other colours. Each of the colours is given a value from 0 (no colour present) to 255 (full intensity). RGB works in the opposite way to CMYK as colours are added together to create a lighter colour. When all three are fully combined the colour white is created. The RGB colour system relies on black being the base colour and adding the colours to it. Figure 2.24 shows the RGB colour combinations for eight colours.

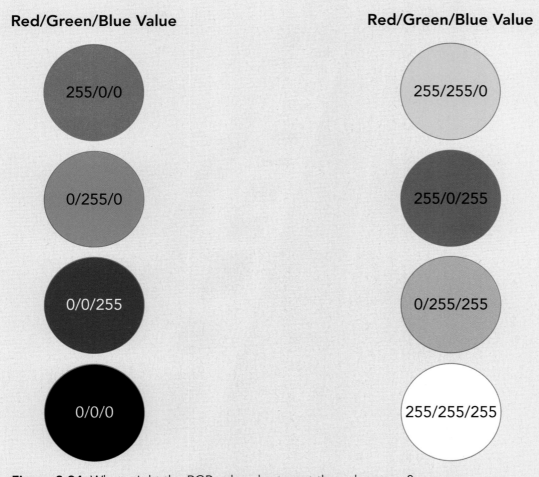

Red/Green/Blue Value

255/0/0

0/255/0

0/0/255

0/0/0

Red/Green/Blue Value

255/255/0

255/0/255

0/255/255

255/255/255

Figure 2.24: What might the RGB values be to get the colour grey?

RGB is the primary colour system for digitally presented media. This is due to the pixels in the screens in devices using a red, green and blue light source.

Use of white space

White spaces are the areas on a page or canvas where space is intentionally left blank. This includes the space between paragraphs, images and other elements on the page. It is important to understand that 'white' space can be any colour though.

Good use of white space makes a graphic design easier to understand. Allowing for space between text means it is easier to comprehend as the content is easier to read. This is referred to as micro white spaces. There are also macro white spaces. These are where the different elements on a page, canvas or web page are laid out to guide the audience to easily go from one element to another.

It is important to use white space properly on a graphic. Too much white space can make the graphic feel sparse and audiences' eyes may not take in the content as it was intended. Too little white space and the audience can feel overwhelmed by the content and struggle to understand the concept or ideas.

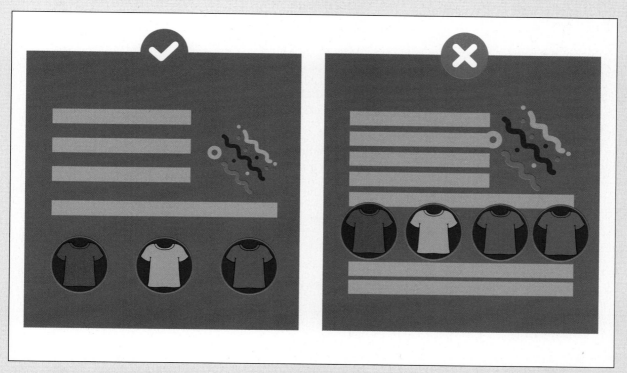

Figure 2.25: Why does effective white space make a graphic easier to understand?

Stretch 1

Many economy brands use very little white space in their advertising, choosing to show off as many products as possible. High-end brands choose to use a lot of white space on their advertisements.

1 Describe the possible reasons for why high-end brands use more white space on their advertisements than economy brands.

2 Explain why white space is necessary on a digital graphic.

3 Analyse the impact both poor and effective use of white space can have on a digital graphic.

Layout conventions for different graphic products

Graphic products take a variety of formats and have a range of purposes. Some are used to inform audiences while others may be used to advertise. However, there are common conventions across many of them. Some examples are given in Table 2.7.

Table 2.7: Layout conventions for different graphic products

Convention	Description
Title	Name of the publication, article or product
Masthead	Located at the top of a page and will often include the title of the publication or the logo. It has the name of the publication such as the name of the magazine or newspaper
Headline	Very short but informative hook for the reader
Copy	Refers to the written elements on the graphic product
Image content	Photos, diagrams or other visual elements that add information and/or interest Cover images are often used to make an instant impact, whatever the format
Additional information	Not essential to the main aim of the page, but included for depth and breadth, e.g. links to webpages

Advertisements

Advertisements are used to promote a product to a target audience. They generally consist of a large title, which may be the product name, to grab the audience's attention. There will often be an image or graphic of the product being promoted. The copy will contain information about the product, stating what it is and what its unique features are. Finally, additional information may be located at the bottom of the advert. This could be terms and conditions or contact information about the business or brand.

Figure 2.26: What layout conventions has this advert used?

CD, DVD and Blu-ray covers

CD, DVD and Blu-ray covers all follow a very similar format. In Figure 2.27, on the next page, you can see how they utilise the various layout conventions.

Copy

Masthead to inform audience of the content

Title

Additional information, e.g. legal, Dolby sound and format

Image content helps draw audience's attention

Figure 2.27: Can you think of any other DVD/Blu-ray covers that share a similar layout to the one above?

Most DVD covers have the same layout conventions. Blu-ray covers share similar conventions with DVDs and much of the time the same set of graphics and layout are used for DVD and Blu-ray covers.

Games

Game case artwork often follows a similar layout to CD/DVD/ Blu-ray covers, because size is a common constraint. Consistent positioning of information also helps consumers and users to find information quickly.

Over to you!   3

1   Compare and contrast the information on these game cases.

   a   What do they have in common and what is different?

   b   How does the layout convey information and 'sell' the game?

2   Review the game boxes against Figure 2.27. What are the similarities and differences?

Figure 2.28: Are there any game cases that you can think of that do not follow any usual conventions displayed in the image above?

Leaflets and posters

Leaflets are a page folded in half two or three times. Their purpose is to promote or give further information and details about a brand or product. The front section of a leaflet will often have the title of the business or product brand it is promoting and relevant graphics, such as the brand logo indicating the product or service. It will aim to capture the audience's attention.

Copy: The key messages the leaflet needs to communicate

Title: Clear indication of the leaflet content

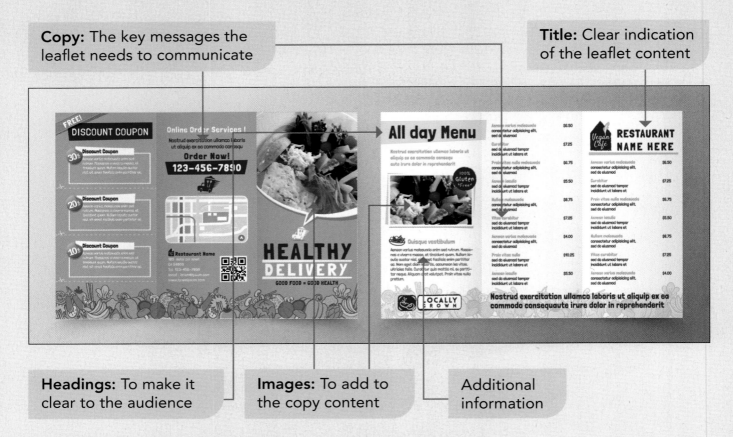

Headings: To make it clear to the audience

Images: To add to the copy content

Additional information

Figure 2.29: Most leaflets are laid out quite similarly, but there may be small differences depending on its purpose. Why is the main content of a leaflet on the inside?

The back of a leaflet may also have contact information for the business or brand such as a phone number, email address or social media accounts. There may also be space for prices or a short paragraph about the business or product brand. This depends on the overall intention for the leaflet.

Posters also follow general layout conventions. The title is often in the largest font size, there is a big image or number of graphics to grab the audience's attention and further information is laid out in a logical manner around these two assets. Usually contact details for a company or terms and conditions are at the bottom of a poster in a small font size. The purpose of a poster is to convey a message to an audience, though this can be done in many ways depending on the business or product brand.

Over to you! 4

Carry out some desk research.

1 Find an example of a poster promoting a restaurant.

2 Compare the leaflet in Figure 2.29 with the poster.

3 What are the similarities and differences?

4 Which one is more effective at communicating its message and why?

Magazine and book covers

Magazines follow very conventional layout rules. The masthead almost always has the title in it to ensure that audiences can clearly see the name of the publication. Various headlines are usually placed around the left and right sides of the page, allowing the audience to quickly see what articles will be in the magazine. The headlines on the left side are particularly important as when magazines are displayed on a shelf, they often overlap each other. In the centre of the page will often be an image of the key person or topic that is the focus of that edition.

Books are more varied in their design. However, most still follow key rules. The front of the book will usually have the title and author. It may also include a subtitle and possibly a positive extract from a review. The image used on the book's front cover is very important as it will be the first element the audience will see; it needs to capture what the book is about. The title of the book will often be in a large font and will be in a typeface that is in keeping with the themes of the book. The back cover of a book will have the blurb, a short summary of the book, the barcode and sometimes a brief description of the author.

Both magazines and books have a spine. If the magazine or book is thick enough the spine will have the title of the product and the author, making it easy to see what they are when on a shelf.

Multimedia products, web images and graphics

Multimedia products involve combining text, audio, images, video and animation to help audiences in various ways. Examples include:

*   order points in restaurants

*   cash machines

*   information points in shopping centres or museums.

Figure 2.30 shows an example of a multimedia product screen in a restaurant setting.

Figure 2.30: Why do multimedia products such as this one need graphics and images?

Web images and graphics are often vector based. They are used to simplify otherwise more complicated graphics. This is useful to customers as they can quickly understand what products or services a business or brand offers. They usually have little copy on them to ensure as many people as possible can understand them. Icons such as those in Figure 2.31 can be used to make it very clear to customers the products that businesses or brands sell.

Figure 2.31: Why are icons more useful than text for people visiting a foreign country on holiday?

Packaging

Packaging can come in many different forms and for many different products. Often packaging will make very clear what the product is with a title, image(s) and concise copy to ensure the audience understands quickly what the product contains.

The purpose of the packaging will have an impact on its physical design. Sometimes packaging is created for a practical use to the product, such as a burger box that may open to also act as a plate. In other situations, packaging is purely for transport uses, such as boxes to carry other products. Usually, the packaging of a product will try to support the advertisement of a product as much as possible.

Let's get creative!

Research different packaging for different products:

- toothpaste
- coffee
- cereal.

How do each of the products ensure they are easily recognisable by customers but still stand out from the competition?

Now create your own packaging for one of the products you have researched; you can be as creative as you want. You must change the type of packaging used though: for example, if the cereal came in a box, you could design cereal packaging in the form of a bag.

Test your knowledge   1

1. Describe the different layout convention elements.

2. Explain how the same element may be used differently depending on the product.

3. Choose a graphic product from the ones mentioned in this section. Redesign the product into another format – for example, a book cover to a DVD cover or poster to magazine cover. Make sure that you stick to the layout conventions for the product you are redesigning.

2.2 Properties of digital graphics and use of assets

Images and graphics are created and stored in digital devices. To humans they can be visually fantastic graphic designs; however, to a computer, they are merely data. It is important to understand the technical properties of digital graphics and the different ways these assets can be used in media products.

Technical properties of images and graphics

There are two different types of image, **bitmap/raster** and **vector**, both of which are covered in this section.

Each graphic type has benefits and drawbacks. The type of graphic a designer may choose to create will depend on the content they have been asked to produce and the purpose of the final asset or product. Usually, logos are created using vector graphics while 'real-life' content will be done in bitmap/raster formats.

Bitmap and raster properties

Bitmap/raster graphics consist of pixels, which are tiny squares of colour. The canvas size will be set to be a certain number of pixels high and wide. This will allow for a bitmap/raster graphic to be created. The more pixels that are available, the better quality the final graphic as there is more capacity for detail. Bitmap/raster graphics are often used on graphic products that require a lot of detail, such as photographs.

Colour depth

When creating a bitmap/raster digital graphic each pixel will have several **bits** available to it that colours can be assigned to. A bit is a value, 0 or 1, that a computer uses to represent data. The more bits available for each pixel, the more colours can be used and the better the overall quality of the image. Table 2.8 shows the number of colours available for each bit.

Table 2.8: Number of colours available for each bit

Number of bits	Number of possible colours
1	2
2	4
4	16
8	256
16	65 536
24	16 777 216

If a pixel has one bit available, the value can be either 0 or 1. This allows for two colours. If a pixel has two bits available, the values can be 00, 01, 10 or 11. This allows for four colours to be used. It is important to remember that the more colours that are used per pixel, the bigger the file size and the better the image quality.

Colour mode

When creating digital graphics, it is important to know the final use of the asset. If the asset is to be used on a digital **platform** such as a website the settings will need to be in RGB. If it is being printed, then it will need to be in CMYK. It is possible to swap the colour modes of a bitmap/raster graphic once it has been created. This means that graphic designers do not need to produce the same graphic in a different colour mode.

Bitmap/raster graphics can also be created in grayscale. This converts the image to black, white and shades of grey. This can be useful as grayscale can give an image a completely different look. Converting to grayscale also saves on storage space.

Compression settings

Large files of any type may sometimes need to have their size reduced, so that they take up less storage space, transfer or upload more quickly or attached to an email. This is called **compression** and is where unnecessary data is deleted from the original image. It should not be confused with making the dimensions (height and width) of an image smaller. Applying compression to an image will decrease the file size but also have an impact on the quality of the image.

File compression is discussed in this section with respect to bitmap and raster graphics, but it can equally be used for other types of static image, moving image and audio files.

When saving bitmap/raster graphics the image editing software often gives users the choice to apply compression. At one end of the scale there is as much compression as possible. This would make the file size very small, possibly 10 per cent to 20 per cent of the original file size. The quality of the image will be impacted though: **artifacts** or pixelation may occur in the image.

On the other end of the scale no compression would be applied. The image retains all its quality but the file size is much bigger in comparison to full compression being applied.

There are two types of compression which can be chosen to reduce the size of images when saving them: **lossy** and **lossless**. These two options can be understood by thinking about speed of load time versus quality of image.

- **Lossy compression:** Some data from the original file is lost when using lossy compression, and you will not be able to get it back without specialist software. Human eyes cannot really spot the difference between lossy and lossless images, so this can be a useful tool for websites, apps and interactive multimedia products because lossy compression reduces the file size considerably. There will be a reduction in quality however, so where image resolution is important, lossless compression should be considered instead.

- **Lossless compression:** Reduces an image's file size without any loss in quality at all. It is done by only taking away any bits of data that are not necessary in the file, leaving those that are directly related to the quality of the image. The compression will not be as much as in a lossy compressed image, so file sizes will be bigger, but the quality will stay the same as the original image.

Figure 2.32: In what ways does compression have an impact on the final quality of an image?

The amount of compression applied will be partly dependent on the final use of the graphic. If it is to be printed out a low amount of compression will need to be applied as these images have a higher pixels per inch value compared to digital images. A digital graphic may be able to have more compression applied to it before it is noticeable due to it being viewed on a screen and so needs a smaller pixel per inch value. There is often a sensible compromise between quality and file size that can be settled on for digital graphics.

Overall quality

One issue with bitmap/raster images is pixelation. This is where an image has been made larger than it was originally created. Often this is caused when a graphic was created with a small canvas size and the graphic is made larger than it was originally intended to be. It is important to think ahead and consider what the bitmap/raster graphic may be used for in the future. If it is not made large enough, issues can occur when it is used in other products.

Figure 2.33 shows an example of when an image has become pixelated due to being made too large.

Figure 2.33: What can be done to minimise pixelation in an image?

The colour depth also needs to be considered when discussing the quality of bitmap/raster graphics. If the colour depth is too low then the final graphic may not be as effective as it might otherwise have been. It will not have as much detail as it would if the colour depth were higher.

When creating digital graphics, designers are always managing the quality of the image in relation to the file size. A bitmap/raster graphic can have a high colour depth and be large in dimensions, but this may create a file size that is not storage space effective.

Transparency

Some bitmap/raster file types support **transparency**. Transparency allows the main graphic to have no background, which is useful for graphical elements such as logos. If transparency is used, the graphical element can be used on other **graphical products**, such as leaflets or posters, while the graphic can make use of the existing background. If Figure 2.34 had a transparent background it could be reused against different colours, adding another use for the image and creating a different graphic.

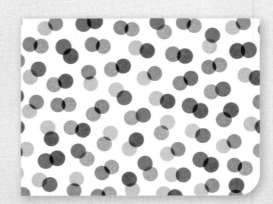

Figure 2.34: For what purposes could this image be used if it had a transparent background?

It is important to remember that not all bitmap/raster file types have the potential for transparency, however. This must be considered when creating a digital graphic.

Test your knowledge   2

1   Why does the number of pixels and colours in bitmap/raster images impact on the file size?

2   What benefits do bitmap/raster images have?

3   What limitations do bitmap/raster images have?

Vector graphic properties

Vector images are very different to bitmap/raster graphics. Instead of creating graphics based on pixels, they use a series of points and paths. Two or more points are set, and a path is put in place between the points. The path can be manipulated so it is straight or curved. Vectors are very useful for graphics that do not need lots of detail, such as logos.

Figure 2.35 shows examples of how points and paths are used to create a simple vector line.

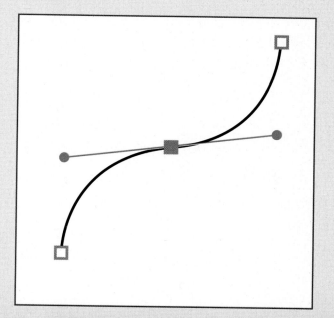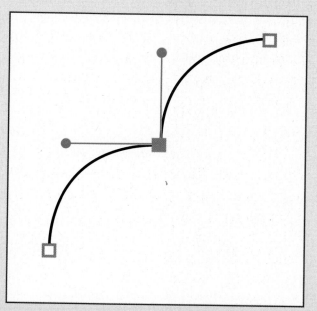

Figure 2.35: What kind of graphics can be created using vectors?

Compatibility and software support

To edit vector graphics specialist software is needed. This is because the process needed to create vector images is completely different to bitmaps/rasters. The final file type of a vector graphic is also uncommon but to work around this limitation, vector graphics are often created in specialist software and converted to bitmap/raster file types. However, the new format graphic no longer has the benefits of a vector graphic.

File size

Unlike bitmap/raster graphics, the file size of a vector image is comparatively very small. This is because far less information needs to be stored. Bitmap/raster graphics need to store the detail for every single individual pixel. Vector graphics only need to store the points and paths. The dimensions of a vector image do not directly relate to the file size of a vector graphic; this means that there can be very big vector graphics that are very small in file size.

Scalability

As vector graphics are based on points and paths, they are easily **scalable** and do not get pixelated like bitmap/raster graphics do. This is very useful when graphics need to be made much bigger than originally planned, such as if printing off for a billboard.

Figure 2.36 shows an example of what happens to vector and bitmap/raster graphics when they are enlarged.

Vector graphics can also be made much smaller in size and still not lose detail and quality. This is especially advantageous for graphics such as logos and brand names, which may need to be large enough to fit on the side of a building but also need to be small enough to fit on items such as pin badges or carrier bags.

Figure 2.36: Why might you choose a vector graphic instead of a bitmap/raster graphic?

Stretch   2

Compare the benefits and limitations of bitmap/raster and vector graphics. Ensure you cover the following points.

1   Which graphic format is best used for which different purposes of digital graphics?

2   What unique features does each graphic format have?

3   In what ways could a designer utilise both formats in a digital graphic?

Licences and permissions to use assets

When using digital graphics and images designers may choose to create their own. There are occasions where existing assets may be used; this could be to save time or because there is an existing asset that suits the designer's needs. Often these assets will have **licences** or permissions attached to them. Graphics with licences or permissions attached may be copyright. See Unit R093, Topic Area 3, 'Intellectual property rights' to learn more about this topic.

Once the graphics or images to be used have been collected, all the information for each graphic and image would be logged in an asset table. This is a document which would have the reference of the graphic or image, its source (where it was located from), if it is copyright and what permissions need to be sought from the owner, such as payment or asking them if the graphic or image can be used for the intended purpose.

Client images and photographs

Clients may have taken images for a designer to use; these could be photographs of their products or work environment. To learn about the privacy and permissions issues involved in using client images see Unit R093, Topic Area 3, 'Privacy and permissions'.

A designer may choose to take their own photographs to use for their client. The designer would retain all rights to these images, unless otherwise specified in their contract, as they are the ones who will have taken the photographs.

Internet images

There are many thousands of images on the internet that might be suitable for use. Search engine filters can help to make the process quicker and easier. Size, image type and licence type are useful criteria to search by.

Size

If you know the dimensions of the final graphical product, you can search for images that meet the size you need, so that you don't need to trawl through images that are too big or too small.

Image type

Another filter that can be applied is image type. Images can be a variety of different types, such as clip art, vectors or GIFs (moving images). Each of these images have different uses. For example, using the vector type would filter out all bitmap/raster graphics. GIFs would only be relevant if the product was on a digital platform such as a website as they have moving elements to them.

Licence type

Another filter that can be applied is by type of licence. As mentioned before images may have copyright attached to them, but they may also have a Creative Commons (CC) licence. Using an asset that has a CC licence saves the designer time as they do not have to gain licences or permissions as they would if they were to use a copyrighted asset. See Unit R093, Topic Area 3, 'Using copyrighted materials' for more about the CC licence.

Logos

Client-owned logos can be used without permission, but if the designer wanted to use a third-party logo they would need to seek permission. This may include logos for famous brands such as Coca-Cola or Nike. This can be very expensive, especially if the business or brand is known worldwide.

Stock library images

Stock library images are very useful for designers to use as there are many photos to use. Most stock library websites use two different types of licence: rights managed and royalty free.

Rights managed

Rights managed images usually have more restrictions than royalty free. These restrictions could include:

- which geographic location(s) the images can be used in
- how many times the image can be used
- how long the image can be used for.

Rights managed licences may also be exclusive. This means that only one person can buy the rights to the image and they alone can use it. To purchase this type of licence can be very expensive. There are also non-exclusive licences, which means anyone can purchase rights to the image and lots of people can use it at the same time.

Royalty free

Royalty free licences usually mean that once a person has purchased the rights to the image, they can use it for as long as they want to. While they do not have the same restrictions as rights managed images, they may still come with several restrictions, such as:

- for non-commercial uses only
- limiting the number of times the image can be printed/used.

Generally, stock library images must also be used as part of a wider project and not on their own. For example, an image should be used alongside other items and not on its own.

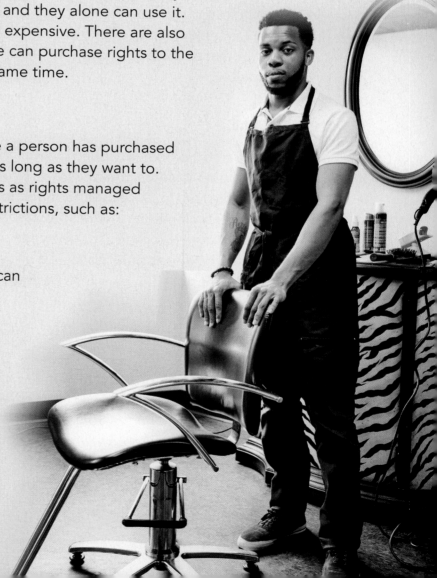

2.3 Techniques to plan visual identity and digital graphics

It is important that before creating any visual identity or digital graphics, they are properly and thoughtfully planned out. Design teams will use a variety of different pre-production documents to plan out their potential creations. Even the planning stage of a project has multiple steps that need to be completed.

Mood board

The purpose of a mood board is to visually represent a theme, feel or idea using images, fonts, colours, materials and even sounds and video. Mood boards are generally in landscape format and contain a collage of different overlapping elements. They allow for collections of ideas to be collated onto a central location for everyone in the team to use. This helps design teams develop the basis of a visual identity or digital graphic. Not all the ideas or themes will be utilised, but the mood board allows for creativeness to be encouraged.

Physical mood board

You can create a physical mood board by hand, cutting and sticking examples onto a board or piece of paper that represent the idea that needs to be communicated. Images, fonts and colours could come from magazines, flyers, posters, adverts, swatches of material, photos and images printed from the internet.

Figure 2.37: Why would other items, such as text, colours and even textiles be important when creating a digital graphic?

Digital mood board

Digital mood boards are like physical ones, but they are created using software such as Microsoft PowerPoint or Adobe Photoshop, online graphic design software such as Canva and Photopea or mood boarding apps. These mood boards can include digitally downloaded fonts along with GIFs, sound effects, soundscapes or ambient noises embedded, and even video clips. However, if you then needed to print it out, those interactive elements would be lost.

Figure 2.38: A mood board that could be used for an advert. What else could be added to it?

Appropriate uses of a mood board

A mood board is generally appropriate to use at a time when initial ideas need generating or visual inspiration is needed. It can be a highly effective tool when used at the beginning of a project to gather a wide range of information or examples to study. It is not an effective document for making any detailed plans and cannot contain too much written information otherwise it becomes too complex and loses its visual impact. Table 2.9 shows the uses for a mood board.

Table 2.9: Uses for a mood board. Can you think what image types might be included for each use?

Context	Use
Idea development	One person creates a mood board to present an idea or concept to others.
Gain inspiration	Creatives work as a team to add sources of inspiration to one mood board.
Develop a look, tone or feel for a product	A mood board is created of products and events that have a similar look, tone or feel to the one the creative team are trying to achieve. This could be shown to the client.
Competitors	Similar products from competitors could be added to a mood board to get a feel for what is in the market already, and how to stand out from the crowd.
Target audience	If a target audience has been clearly defined, a mood board can help designers to present images of target audience interests, likes and trends.

To improve a mood board's effectiveness, you need to relate the content directly to the brief and focus on one aspect of that brief. A single mood board should not be used to cover all aspects of a brief and should be adapted to fit the context.

A project to create a new children's eBook, for example, would not require a mood board presenting images of all children's eBooks on the market already for all ages and genres. Instead, a mood board could be narrowed down to show images of the interests of a specific target audience within the 'children's' category or specific genre of children's eBook.

Mind map

A mind map is a diagram created to support ideas generation and organise information. The purpose of a mind map is to help plan and organise thoughts and ideas so that they can be developed further. This visual method also makes it easier for other people to see a designer's thought process and contribute to it.

It will contain a main idea or concept that is drawn in the middle of the diagram inside a box, circle or other shape called a **node**. Coming away from the main idea, will be associated ideas that are in shapes called sub-nodes, linked to the main idea via lines known as branches. Those sub-nodes will all have their own branches and further sub-nodes attached to them, and so on until the idea has been exhausted and a useful level of detail has been achieved.

Physical mind map

At its most basic level, a mind map can be completed using only a pencil, rubber and paper. Typically, you would start by writing the main idea down, then adding in each new sub-node, as you think of it. You can follow one node, adding in more branches and detail to the very end, or you can choose to create several sub-nodes first, then develop them a stage further, and continue on until all ideas have been exhausted.

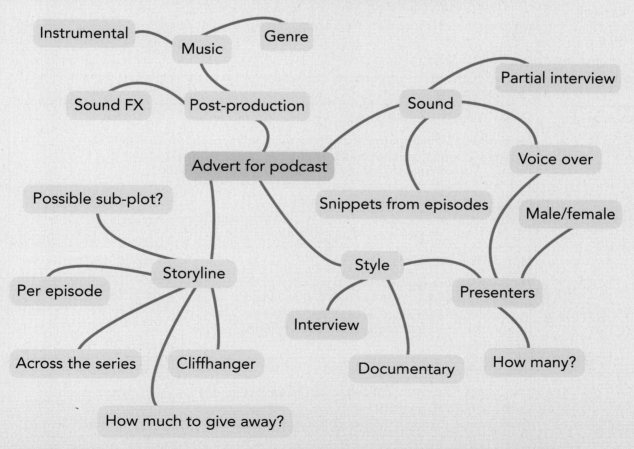

Figure 2.39: Can you think of any additional nodes or sub-nodes to add onto this mind map?

Digital mind map

Mind maps can also be created using computer software such as presentation software like Microsoft PowerPoint or Keynote. There are also mind mapping websites and apps that can be downloaded and used that include colour, images and even emojis. See Figure 1.37 (BBFC issues) in Unit R093, Topic Area 3, 'Classification systems and certifications'.

Appropriate uses of a mind map

While any individual can use a mind map as a planning tool, one of the most useful ways it can be used is by groups of designers or creatives who need to come up with an idea together. Each team member can contribute to the mind map and this often helps the group of contributors to come to a joint decision. Mind maps are not generally used with a client as they are more focused towards the initial planning of a project or design. Table 2.10 shows how mind maps can be used.

Table 2.10: Uses of mind maps and examples

Use	Mind map content	Who is it useful for?
Summarising genre or content requirements for a media product	**Main node:** Genre and content **Sub-nodes:** Different aspects of the chosen genre, colours, imagery, content requirements from the brief along with notes on all of the options	Designers Creative team
Idea generation	**Main node:** Ideas **Sub-nodes:** Idea 1, idea 2, idea 3, etc. with branches from each of these outlining aspects of each idea	Designers Creative team, client
Planning	**Main node:** Name of project **Sub-nodes:** Pre-production, production and distribution stages, branches from these detailing actions that need to happen at each stage, with further branches detailing who could complete each action. This could then inform the workplan	Creative team, technical team, senior roles, anyone who is involved in the smooth running of the project
Audience research collation	**Main node:** Audience research **Sub-node:** Split into **qualitative** and **quantitative**, then split further into primary and secondary with branches to sub-nodes detailing the types of research undertaken	Creative team Distribution team Senior roles

Table 2.10: Continued

Use	Mind map content	Who is it useful for?
Creative thinking to solve a problem	**Main node:** Problem faced **Sub-node:** A breakdown of the problem into its component parts, with branches to possible solutions	Creative team Distribution team Senior roles
Taking notes in client meetings	**Main node:** Client meeting or product name **Sub-node:** A new sub-node every time there is a new topic in the meeting, with branches to all the content discussed	Client Creative team
Thinking through complex pre-production or production scenarios	**Main node:** Pre-production or production issue **Sub-node:** Different steps that need to be taken for the situation to be successful	Technical team Senior roles Producer

A mind map is such an effective planning tool because it allows you to think both across a project but also to drill down into certain aspects too. It allows you to exhaust a possibility to see if it is workable or to introduce several different ideas at the same level. Mind mapping will often result in the team knowing what their next step needs to be.

A mind map's effectiveness can be improved when the content of it is specific and relevant to the context. For example, there is no point generating a mind map discussing different possible target audiences for a product when the client brief clearly already says who the desired target audience is.

Concept sketch

Concept sketches are used to show roughly what products or designs may look like. They are not used solely for digital graphics; they are also used in other design-based industries such as architecture. Once a rough idea has been created, a designer will create a concept sketch. From here the sketch will be critiqued; what works and should stay in the design and what needs to be changed or is not needed. This cycle would happen until the team are happy with the final design.

When the final design has been agreed, the next step of the process would take place and renderings of the digital graphic or product would start to be created. These would look like the final product.

Figure 2.40: What other industries can you think of that use concept sketches?

Visualisation diagrams

Visualisation diagrams share some similarities with concept sketches but they are more focused towards digital graphic products such as magazine covers, posters or advertisements.

Visualisation diagrams are used to create a rough idea of what a graphic product might look like. They will show design ideas, for example what style the product might use and usually also show the layout of the product. For example, a poster advert for a supermarket will be created as a visualisation diagram first to give the design team a rough idea of the final product.

The visualisation diagram would also include annotations. These would be to help label different aspects of the visualisation diagram, for example the title or any images. However, the annotations may also include details that are less tangible, such as the reasoning behind their ideas. This type of annotation would help ensure that everyone in the creative and technical teams know the explanations behind the designs and decisions made.

An effective visualisation will be clear and detailed. Artistic talent is not necessarily required to create a useful visualisation diagram, just the ability to accurately portray all the elements a graphic designer may need to create the media product from it. Hand drawn sketches are often used, but they can also be created digitally using graphic design or presentation software.

To improve a visualisation diagram's effectiveness, you must make sure that the content is obvious and relevant. For example, instead of including the word 'title' where the title of a DVD cover should go, the actual title of the DVD should be included using the style and size of font required.

Figure 2.41: Why would there have been a visualisation diagram created for this comic page before being made in image editing software?

Case study

ITV rebrand

The TV channel ITV underwent a brand redesign in 2013. The old design was very formal and needed bringing up-to-date with the new brand values.

ITV's design team joined forces with an external design studio and work began on planning out the new visual identity. The team started with mind maps based around their core values, types of programming they put out and what their vision for the channel was. From there ITV's design team took these concepts and ideas and started to create a new visual identity.

The design team used the existing mind maps and created mood boards to help them with the creative process; they involved colours, different typefaces and key words. These would prove very useful throughout the process as if they were struggling for inspiration they were able to refer back to the mood boards.

Figure 2.42: Why would a designer create multiple versions of the same logo?

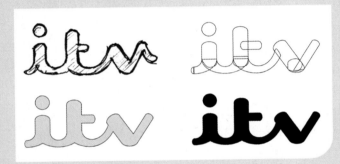

Figure 2.43: What pre-production document might these graphics have been put on to help generate ideas?

Their new logo was designed to be modern and cool; it went as simple as possible, just retaining the letters ITV but in a unique typeface. The design team created concept sketches of the logo to help them visualise their ideas.

Finally, after all the planning, the logo was completed. The final version was colourised, and the colours reflected the network's wide range of programming, but it was also able to be used in black and white. The graphic created was a true reflection of what ITV wanted to be known for: a modern, diverse and inclusive brand.

Check your understanding

1   Describe how each of the four pre-production documents could be used to create and develop ideas with digital graphics.

2   Explain the benefits of planning projects out before starting them.

3   Evaluate the usefulness of concept sketches when compared to visualisation diagrams: where would each one be used and why?

Review your learning

Test your knowledge   3

1 Why are vector graphics useful for logos?

2 Explain the benefits of vector graphics in terms of file size.

3 Analyse where vector graphics and bitmap/raster graphics may be used:

   a give examples of graphic products where each would be used

   b explain why the other format would not be used or why it is not as suitable.

What have you learnt?

		See section
•	Graphic design and conventions.	2.1
•	Properties of digital graphics and use of assets.	2.3
•	Techniques to plan visual identity and digital graphics.	2.3

Create visual identity and digital graphics

Let's get started

What image editing tools do you know about? How do you think digital graphics or images can be manipulated?

What will you learn?

- Tools and techniques of imaging editing software used to create digital graphics.

- Technical skills to source, create and prepare assets for use within digital graphics.

- Techniques to save and export visual identity and digital graphics.

3.1 Tools and techniques of imaging editing software used to create digital graphics

Digital graphics can be made in many ways. Most often they are created or edited in **image editing software** such as Adobe Photoshop, GIMP, PaintShop Pro or Photopea. While the presentation of the software looks different, the functionality of them is largely the same. You need to be aware of the different tools and techniques the software offers and be able to choose the correct tool or technique.

Image and canvas size

All digital images have a size; this can be in computer dimensions such as pixels or physical measurements like centimetres, millimetres or inches. When creating a digital graphic, it is important to check the canvas is the correct size. If it is too small then the final graphic may not be usable for its intended purpose. If the canvas size is too large then the final image may take up unnecessary storage space on a digital device.

When creating a new canvas, the first step is to set up its size. This is dependent on the purpose of the asset to be created. Users need to know if they are creating a digital graphic for a product that will be displayed digitally or one that will be printed out physically. Each has a different **pixels per inch (PPI)** value and the user will set the PPI count before creating their digital graphic. A printed product will need to be created with a higher PPI count than a digital product. This is because when products are printed, they can look pixelated or blurry if a lower PPI count is used in the digital graphics file. Table 2.11 shows the different industry standard PPI values for digital and printed products.

Table 2.11: The different PPI values for digital or printed products

PPI industry standard options	Asset type	Example uses
72	Digital	Web-page images
300	Physical	Posters, leaflets, magazine covers

Figure 2.44: How can the number of pixels per inch impact on the quality of an image? (150 PPI is shown to illustrate the difference between 72 PPI and 300 PPI)

It is important to create the canvas in the correct size and PPI value as otherwise the asset produced will look odd if it was used for an alternative purpose. It is possible with most image editing software to change the canvas or image size, and to make the canvas bigger or smaller if the digital graphic requires it.

Layout tools

To help users ensure their graphics follow the shape or style they want, they may use layout tools including grids, guides and rulers. Each tool has its own purpose to help graphic designers ensure they get the end product they wanted.

Grids

Grids are used to ensure that different graphic elements such as shapes or typography are placed in the right location on the canvas. They separate the canvas into equal sections and are usually square or rectangular and are generated by the program itself. However, the graphic designer can set how far they want each gridline to be from each other. There is generally an option to 'snap' objects to the grid. This is useful if the user wants to ensure all their graphic elements stay aligned with each other.

Guides

Guides are like grids – however the user can create all the guidelines themselves. This is beneficial if the graphic designer has a particular idea they want to implement and needs to use a non-conventional layout that is not provided by grids.

Rulers

Rulers can help graphic designers ensure that the size of their assets are correct in comparison to the canvas or page size. Rulers also determine a grid or guides origin point. The origin point of a ruler can be changed, for example if the user wants to add a margin to a canvas or page.

Drawing tools

There are a variety of different drawing tools that can be used in image editing software. Digital graphics such as logos are created using a combination of these drawing tools.

Shapes

The shapes drawing tool allows a graphic designer to create basic shapes such as rectangles or circles, to make their own shapes or use a pre-set selection of shapes and edit them further to suit their purpose. When users combine shapes together they can create different assets, such as logos or abstract shapes, that can be used in other digital graphics. Shapes can also be manipulated using the transform tool, which allows for new shapes to be created in a variety of different ways. This can help the user create the asset they were looking for.

Figure 2.45: What shapes have been combined to create each of these numbers?

Colour fill and gradients

Two other tools often used with shapes are the colour fill and gradient tools. The colour fill tool fills a shape with a single block of colour. The gradient tool allows for two or more colours to be used in a shape; the colours will gently blend into each other.

The use of each tool depends on the purpose of the final product. For example, text is generally easier to read with a solid colour fill while the background of a poster may use a gradient fill to help contrast with the other assets on the graphic.

Let's get creative!   1

A new airline company, Blue Skies, has been set up and needs a new logo for their visual identity. Complete the following tasks.

- Use and manipulate shapes to create a logo for the company.

- Once you have created the logo, experiment with different fill and gradient effects.

Adjustments to images

There are a variety of different adjustments that can be made to digital graphics within image editing software. Some of the adjustments create large changes to images while others are more subtle but just as effective.

Brightness and contrast

The brightness of an image is in relation to how much light is given out, and this varies between images. Turning the brightness up on an image will make the overall image become lighter while turning the brightness down will make the image darker. Setting the brightness higher can help bring out certain elements of a digital graphic that might be more difficult to see if the brightness was lower.

Contrast is the difference between the maximum and minimum intensity of a pixel in an image. When contrast is set higher, the light areas in an image become lighter while the dark areas become darker. Setting the contrast lower will make these differences less obvious.

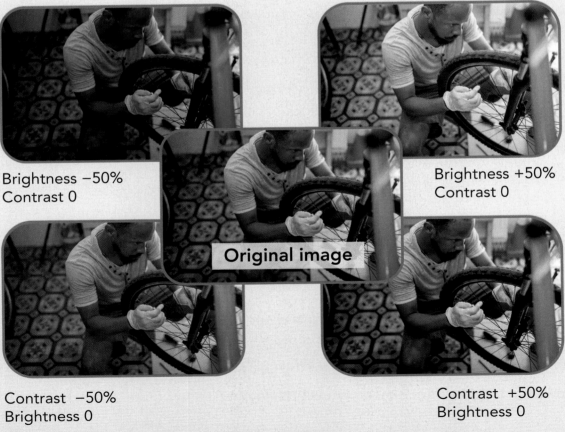

Brightness −50%
Contrast 0

Brightness +50%
Contrast 0

Original image

Contrast −50%
Brightness 0

Contrast +50%
Brightness 0

Figure 2.46: What impact does changing the brightness and contrast have on an image?

Both brightness and contrast should be used carefully. It is very easy to make an image look unnatural by changing the brightness or contrast too much.

Colour

There are several different adjustments that can be made to the colour of digital graphics, including levels, colour balance, hue and saturation.

Levels

Levels make use of the **histogram** of an image. The level tool visually represents the lightest and darkest tones in an image and every tone in between. It allows users to manipulate the lightest and darkest parts of an image. This is like changing the contrast but using levels allows a user to make more fine-tuned adjustments to a digital graphic as they manipulate the histogram of a digital graphic itself.

Colour balance

The colour balance tool can help correct colour issues with an image. This is useful if a graphic designer wants to bring out certain colours more than others or do the opposite. This is done on a scale; small amounts of a set of colours can be added or taken away. Usually just a minor alteration one way or the other can have a big impact on the colour of an image. The colour balance tool can also be used to create drastic changes to images, such as alter the entire image to be based around one colour. Colour balance allows a user to add more of a colour or colours separately. For example, a user can add more red, green or blue to their image to help add in or remove certain colours.

Hue and saturation

The hue and saturation tool is useful when a graphic designer wants to bring colours out further in an image. The hue and saturation tool works on the whole image; it changes all the colours in an image. The hue represents the colour in an image. Changing the hue may result in certain colours being swapped for others, as the value is changed on the colour wheel. The saturation of an image is the intensity of the colour.

Decreasing the saturation will make the colour look faded and less intense. Increasing the saturation will result in an image that is very vivid but may not always look natural.

Over to you! 1

There are two versions of the same image below. One shows the saturation at its original level and the other has the saturation at 0.

Figure 2.47: Can you think of any logos that are only in black and white?

1 Which image is more visually appealing and why?

2 Why is it important for a designer to consider how their designs might look in greyscale?

Like brightness and contrast, the different adjustments that can be made to the colour of an image need to be used carefully. Changing the colour too much may make an image unusable for its intended purpose.

Selection tools

In image editing software there are a variety of tools to select parts or areas of a digital image. Being able to select and edit individual areas of a digital graphic is important as sometimes only small parts of a digital graphic need to be edited. There are several tools that can be used to select part of an image including shapes, the Magic Wand and the Magnetic Lasso.

Shape

One way of selecting a part of an image is using shapes, often referred to as the Marquee tool. As mentioned earlier in the drawing tools section, image editing software usually has in-built shapes such as rectangles or circles that the user can change in dimension. These can be used to select a part of an image, which fits the pre-set shape provided. There is usually an option to add multiple shape selections together meaning that more complex shapes can be selected.

Colour

Another method of selection, using colour, is a tool called the Magic Wand (the name may vary depending on the software program being used). This selection tool will select objects/areas based on the colour. For example, if there were two areas in an image that were the same colour the Magic Wand tool could be used to select both of those areas and they could be edited together.

For more complex images, the tolerance of the Magic Wand can be changed. This will allow a more specific or general area to be selected. It is often useful to change the tolerance in small increments, so the user only selects the correct parts of an image. For example, if a user wanted to choose a small range of shades of one colour, the tolerance would be low. If the user wanted to select a bigger area of one colour, which included more shades, the tolerance would be set higher.

Edge contrast

The last selection tool, which uses edge contrast, is the Magnetic Lasso tool (the name may vary depending on the software program being used). This tool is useful for shapes that the Marquee tool cannot be used for, such as the outline of a person. The user has the ability to place 'anchors', which can be used to trace the outline of the object. When the start and end of the Magnetic Lasso tool meet again it creates an object that is editable. This is very useful if the user wishes to change the background behind a person because they can 'cut' the person out of the original image and place them in a new image.

Layers and layer styles

Layers are an important part of any digital graphic. They allow the separate parts of a digital image to be edited independently of each other. This is beneficial as graphic designers can ensure that they are editing on one part of the graphic without impacting on the other layers. Most digital graphics will have multiple separate layers that, when seen together, will form a complete graphic.

Once a layer has been created, its **opacity** can be changed, making some layers look see-through. This can be used to make assets stand out or fade into the background of a graphic. This allows key parts of one graphic to not be obscured by another asset.

Figure 2.48: What layers can you identify in this image?

Layers can also be merged. This is useful when two or more designs in a graphic have been completed and they can be made into one layer. This is beneficial as special effects such as transparency are kept and any hidden elements to any of the layers are not changed in this process.

It is important to use sensible names for layers so graphic designers can easily understand which layer is which. This is because for some digital graphics there could be many layers, and if they are named in a confusing or ineffective way a user may waste a lot of time looking for the right layer.

Layer styles

Most image editing software includes the ability to add effects to layers, also known as **layer styles**. Layer styles are useful as they are in-built, meaning users do not need to create them, and new styles can often be imported in too. When a layer is created, a user can select it and choose to add a variety of different effects. Several different effects are described in Table 2.12.

Table 2.12: Layer style effects

Style/effect	Description
Drop shadow	Used to make the asset look like it has depth and helps separate an asset from its background.
Glow	Used to highlight the edges of an asset or text in a different colour.
Bevel and emboss	Used to make an asset look like it is raised or depressed.
Colour overlay	Used to apply a tint of colour over the layer.
Gradient overlay	Similar to a colour overlay but more complex as more colours can be used.
Pattern overlay	Similar to a colour and gradient overlay but uses pre-set patterns that have settings that a user can alter.

It is also possible to add textures to layers. This is useful when a user wants to make a graphic look old or add another aspect to a graphic. This process first involves the user finding the texture they want to apply, for example a paper or film grain effect. The user then places the texture onto the graphic and tweaks settings like brightness, contrast, saturation and hue to make the effect more or less noticeable in the graphic.

Retouching

Image editing software is also used to **retouch** and improve existing images. A graphic designer may decide to retouch an existing image that is similar to what they want to use rather than create a new image, because it will save them time. Retouching techniques can be used to remove unwanted elements from an image. There are many different retouching techniques available to users.

Figure 2.49: What impact does this image have on the audience?

Pencil and brush

The pencil and brush tools work similarly to a physical pencil or brush on a canvas. Both tools allow a user to draw on a canvas or image in a colour chosen by them. The effects of these tools can be edited further using basic tools such as the eraser or blur tools. See the section about the blur tool later in this topic.

Despite the pencil and brush tools having similar functions, the result can be very different. The pencil tool will give a very solid result, with the user only being able to change the diameter of the pencil stroke. It has no **anti-aliasing** properties meaning that the end asset can be rough in appearance and so the blur tool may also be needed.

The brush tool has many more options for a user to use. Like the pencil tool, the diameter of the brush stoke can be altered. However, the hardness of the brush can be changed as well. This allows the brush edges to be soft, which gives the appearance of a light touch, or hard, which is similar in style to the pencil tool. However, the brush tool has anti-aliasing properties, so the final asset is always very smooth.

The opacity of the brush can also be changed, which means that the line created can have a level of transparency to it. Finally, the flow of the line can be adjusted, which allows the user to start with a light shade of their chosen colour and make the shade darker if they go over the line again multiple times with the brush tool.

Let's get creative!   2

A new fast-food restaurant specialising in burgers has opened and needs someone to design some assets for them to use at their interactive ordering kiosk.

The business would like you to design the different elements of a burger such as the:

- bottom and top of the bun
- fillings such as lettuce, cheese, gherkins and tomatoes
- burger patty
- sauces such as BBQ, tomato and mustard.

Each element should be on a separate layer and be designed from a bird's eye viewpoint. Use the grid to help you plan your assets.

Use a combination of shapes, the brush tool, fills and gradients to make the different elements look as good as possible.

Cloning

The clone tool is very useful as it allows users to recreate one area of an image in another. This is often used to add further details to an image by replicating one area in another. A source point needs to be identified first; this is the area the user wants to copy. Once the source point has been identified a user can use the clone tool like a brush and copy it over the target area. Once done, selection tools may be used to remove any unwanted parts of the cloned area.

Healing

The healing tool, often called the healing brush, allows for small blemishes or imperfections to be removed, often giving a cleaner look to an image. Similar to the clone tool, the healing tool requires a source point to be identified. The healing brush tool will then look at the surrounding area that the user wants to use the tool on and combine both the source point and target area. This results in a smooth heal which blends in well with the original image.

Blur

Using the blur tool allows for additional effects to be applied on a digital graphic. It can help focus an audience's attention on an area of a graphic or give the impression of motion or speed. The blur tool can be also used to help make a digital graphic with two or more assets look smoother or better combined, as it can help to blend in two separate areas.

Figure 2.50: What retouching tools could be used to remove the people from this image?

Stretch

1 Explain, using examples, why the clone and healing brush tools may be used to improve and enhance digital graphics.

2 What other tools and techniques could be applied after these tools to further improve a digital graphic? Explain how each one can improve a digital graphic.

Colour swatches

Colour swatches are a collection of colours used regularly by a graphic designer. They are helpful as they enable a user to use a smaller selection of colours. A user can select a variety of different colours using the colour picker tool and store them in a swatch. Many image editing programs have pre-loaded colour swatches using colour systems like Pantone. Using these swatches ensures that when a product is completed, it will have accurate colour reproduction, for example if it was printed.

Colour picker

The colour picker tool, also known as the eyedropper tool, allows a user to identify the colour of a single pixel, which they can then use with a brush, solid colour fill or as part of a gradient. This is helpful as there are occasions where a user may find the desired shade for their current work in an existing image. Another way it can be used is if a user creates a colour or shade themselves and they want to use it again to ensure consistency in their visual identity.

Typography

Many digital graphics will have some form of text on them, and image editing software often gives graphic designers different ways of editing the text they want to use. A user can write text horizontally or vertically on a canvas or digital image, which allows for more creativity. Like word-processing or presentation software, there are usually many in-built fonts available for users to use. They can change certain elements such as the alignment of the text, apply different emphasis and apply varying methods of anti-aliasing. The size of the text can also be edited and changed to suit the needs to the graphic product being created.

Figure 2.51: How does the direction of text help add interest and variety to this image?

Font styles and sizes

Font styles allow graphic designers to apply textures and colour schemes to fonts. There are usually font styles pre-loaded into image editing software; however, many programs also allow users to install their own fonts downloaded from the internet. Using existing font styles can often save users time as they do not have to edit an existing font to get it how they want. For more about font styles look back at Topic Area 2, 'Typography'. The size of text can also be changed to suit the graphic product.

Font effects

Like layer styles, fonts can be given layer effects to make them stand out more. This is useful when graphic designers need to make a particular heading or title stand out as it helps audiences easily identify what message is trying to be communicated. It is important to remember to use effects on text sparingly as too many effects on a digital graphic can overwhelm the audience and make the graphic look busy.

Filters and effects

Most image editing software has in-built filters and effects that can be applied to digital graphics to quickly change the look of the graphic. These can be very useful for novice users of the software as they can make a digital graphic look very different with minimal effort.

Filters or effects can be used in the following ways on a digital graphic:

- change from colour to greyscale (monochrome)
- alter appearance drastically by applying a wind effect
- change colours so they are more focused around one colour (changing the hue and saturation)
- sharpening or softening an image
- applying a **vignette** to a graphic to help an audience understand the key focus of a digital graphic.

Stylise filters can be used to change the look of a digital graphic. They could make a graphic look like it has a wind effect, to give the appearance of speed, or highlight all the edges in a bright neon glow. These effects should be used sparingly though as they can visually overwhelm the audience.

If a user applies a monochrome effect to an image, it will turn the colours to greyscale. This can be useful if the designer wants to achieve a certain style with their digital graphic. As mentioned previously, users can also change the hue and saturation to enhance an image (colour toning).

To help draw focus to a particular aspect or part of an image, a vignette can be added. This effect fades the background of an image partly or completely. This effect is useful for when a designer wants to ensure that a certain aspect or part of a digital graphic is the focus for the audience.

Let's get creative!   3

Find an image on the internet and save it onto your device.

Investigate and apply the following effects to the image, making sure to save each one separately and re-load the original image before moving onto the next task.

a   Make the image sharper or softer.

b   Change the image from colour to greyscale.

c   Apply a stylised effect to the image.

3.2 Technical skills to source, create and prepare assets for use within digital graphics

It is important that you are aware of how to source, create and prepare assets so they can be used in digital graphic projects.

Sourcing assets

There are a variety of different ways to source assets; however, the most common is using the internet. Images can be found from stock libraries, though these generally also need a licence to be used. Clients themselves may also have a selection of images that they have taken that would be freely available for a designer to use. Sometimes a client would prefer a designer to use their own images, especially if the client has asked the designer to create a visual identity for a specific business or product brand. Search engines can also be used to locate images, and these may be free to use, especially if they have a Creative Commons licence or are licence free.

Creating assets

An asset can be created by a graphic designer on a blank canvas by combining shapes together or digitally drawing shapes with the brush or pencil tool. The graphic designer can create an asset exactly how they want it to look, if they have the relevant artistic skills. These assets would be saved as a bitmap/raster or vector image.

An alternative is to find an existing asset and edit it. See Section 3.1 for more about how graphics can be edited. Using existing assets is very useful to a graphic designer as if they can find something that already exists it will often save a lot of time.

Modifying assets

Once an asset has been sourced and edited, a user needs to ensure that it has **technical compatibility**. There are two main ways in which an asset can be modified to ensure technical compatibility: rasterising and resampling.

Rasterising

It is important to remember that once a vector graphic has been completed it will need to be **rasterised**. This changes a vector graphic into a bitmap image so it can be used. It is useful to keep a copy of the vector file because rasterised assets cannot be turned back into a vector image.

Resampling

A completed digital graphic may need to be **resampled**. In this process image editing software will change the pixels per inch value of an asset so it can be used for either print or digital use.

The pixel dimensions may also be changed, which resizes the asset. For example, if the size of the intended product is much smaller than the original digital graphic, then the pixel dimensions of the graphic would be made smaller.

Storing assets

Any images downloaded from the internet should be properly stored on a device. This means copying them from the default download folder on the device into a dedicated asset folder for each project. Each image or graphic should also be appropriately named to ensure that they are easy to identify. For example, a user may separate images into three folders when they are working on a project:

- **Original images:** Contains the original or unedited versions of an image or graphic.

- **Edited images:** Contains any images that are being edited but are not yet finished.

- **Final versions:** Contains any images that are completed and are ready to be used in a larger graphic product or for distribution.

3.3 Techniques to save and export visual identity and digital graphics

Saving assets

When saving assets, the file format is important. For example, some image file types do not allow for transparency when saving, which results in an image with a black or white background that would need to be removed before it could be used. Formats may also be lossy file types meaning that once saved, compression is applied to the image and data is lost from the original image.

It is best to save files in the most appropriate format for the asset as this can be different on every occasion. To retain the best image quality, a lossless file format would be used; however, these graphics are often large file sizes, which means that a large amount of storage space is needed on the computer or device that is storing them.

Over to you!   **2**

Using one of the digital graphics you have created or sourced from a previous task, test your skills by doing the following to it.

a   Change the pixel density to 300 PPI.

b   Change the dimensions to a different value.

c   Save the file in an alternative format.

Exporting assets

When the time comes to **export** the asset or digital graphic several factors need to be considered.

- What pixels per inch value is needed?

- Does the digital graphic need to have certain dimensions (width or height)?

- Is there a file type for the graphic that would be best suited to the needs of the client?

Once all these factors have been considered the file is ready to be exported in the chosen file type. Often the original file, with the highest quality settings, will be saved securely so it can be edited or exported again if necessary.

Case study

A day in the life of a graphic designer

When a graphic designer starts a new project, they usually follow a standard process to creating digital graphics. Once they have produced or been given pre-production documents such as mind maps, mood boards and possibly a visualisation diagram or concept sketch, they will start on creating the asset or graphic product.

They may use shape or vector tools with a grid or guidelines active on their canvas to help them ensure that the proportions of the design are correct. If they are making a graphic product such as a leaflet or designing an item of packaging, the designer will collect image assets together. These may be from search engines or stock libraries, unless the designer is creating them. The images found will be saved into a folder, with an appropriate naming convention, to make it easier for the designer to locate them.

Figure 2.52: What benefits would a graphics tablet have over a keyboard and mouse for a graphic designer?

Most of the time, all assets to be used will be sourced first and then edited. The brightness, contrast and colour levels may be tweaked, imperfections may be retouched using the healing brush or clone stamp tool and filters could be used to enhance the assets. Once the designer is happy with the edited assets, they will make sure to save them in a folder of the final versions of the assets.

Finally, the designer will start to put the graphic product together, adding all the assets into the product alongside the relevant text in a suitable typography. The completed graphic product will be saved in the most suitable file format or exported into the format required by the client.

Check your understanding

1 Give three reasons to store unfinished and finished assets separately.

2 Describe why logos are often made as vector images.

3 Evaluate the importance of version numbering when working on a project.

Review your learning

Test your knowledge

1   Identify the different methods a graphic designer can use to source an asset.

2   Describe why it is important to save assets with sensible file names and in separate folders.

3   Explain why technical compatibility is needed for digital graphics and how an asset's properties can be changed to ensure technical compatibility.

What have you learnt?

	See section
• Tools and techniques of imaging editing software used to create digital graphics.	3.1
• Technical skills to source, create and prepare assets for use within digital graphics.	3.2
• Techniques to save and export visual identity and digital graphics.	3.3

Glossary

Key terms

Alignment: The process of lining up different elements together so they are easier to read or understand.

Alliteration: Using words which all have the same letter, one after another in the same sentence.

Amplitude: A measurement of the sound wave that is being recorded, at each point it is taken.

Anti-aliasing: The process of ensuring that lines are as smooth as possible in a high-resolution image.

Artifact: In digital media, a flaw or unintentional change that comes from processing techniques.

Asset: Image, graphic, video or sound that needs to be sourced from a third party or created when making a media product.

Attribution: The creator of the asset must be credited/acknowledged if the asset is used.

Bit: A binary value, 0 or 1, that computers use to represent data.

Bit depth: The number of units of data (bits) available for a sound clip.

Brand identity: The collection or complete set of elements a business creates to portray itself to a consumer. It includes the brand's visual identity.

Brand loyalty: A process where over time consumers will continue buying the same product from a specific brand rather than other brands.

Brand positioning: Establishing a brand in a certain price bracket to help consumers identify brands they want to purchase from.

Brand values: The beliefs that a business or product brand stand for.

Canvas: The name given to a digital page where digital graphics can be created.

Catchphrase: A well-known phrase which may be associated with someone famous or with a business or product/service brand.

Chronological order: The time order that events happen in, from first to last.

Classification: The labelling of products based on their suitability for an audience. Once classification has been completed, a certificate will be issued to show that the media product has been approved.

Client: The company or individual who sets the brief for a media product or service.

Client brief: A written document or verbal explanation based on a design idea from a client that gives the requirements for a project. This project will be worked on by creative and technical teams, who will design and build the final product to meet these requirements.

Colour palette: A range of colours available for a graphic designer to use for a particular brand.

Colour system: The process of mixing hues and colours together. Several different colour systems are used in the creation of digital graphics such as Pantone, NCS, CMYK and RBG.

Compression: The reduction in the amount of data or information stored as part of an image file when it is being saved.

Computer game: A digital product in which players interact with objects displayed on a personal computer, games console, arcade machine, tablet or mobile phone.

Computer-generated imagery (CGI): Visual details that are created by a computer program or drawn digitally, to change or enhance the original footage.

Concept design: The earliest stage of the design process, where ideas are outlined to meet a client brief.

Connotations: The ideas and feelings associated with objects, colours and media codes.

Constraint: A limiting factor placed on a project or creative team, that affects the quality and style of the media product that can be made.

Contingencies: Plans made for a possible situation or event that may happen.

Conventions: The method or way something is usually done. In media, the accepted ways that technical, symbolic and written codes might be used. Closely connected to genre and audience.

Copyright: A legal right a creator or copyright holder has to use material as they would like.

Creative Commons: A special type of licence that allows creators to share their work with their own limitations imposed on it.

Defamation: A spoken or written statement that is false and hurts someone's reputation or allows them to be ridiculed or shunned by society.

Demographic: A particular section of the population.

Derivative works: Larger pieces of creative work of which a particular image is one element. Where 'no derivative works' is a requirement of a licence, this means the asset must be used as it is and cannot be edited by a third party, such as a media organisation.

Design: The drafting and refining of ideas for a product.

Distribution: The promotion and delivery of media products to their audiences, both digitally and in physical form.

Dots per inch (DPI): This describes the number of dots of ink or toner cartridge that are printed onto one inch of an image.

eBook: A digital version of a book that is viewed using a computer, tablet, mobile phone or other handheld device.

Export: The process of making a digital graphic ready for its final purpose or use. Usually exported images are not edited (unlike saving an image).

Extras: Volunteer or paid actors who appear in the background of scenes.

Fill lights: The secondary light or lights used in a frame to balance out the key light and lighten any shadows.

Font: A set of printed, typed or hand drawn letters, numbers and symbols which all use the same design style.

Frame rate: The number of images or frames shown per second in a video product.

Graphical elements: Any visual elements on a design, which can include pictures, shapes, logos or typography.

Graphical products: Products such as posters, packaging and BluRay covers that have digital graphics on them.

Health and safety mitigations: Ways in which the risk of health and safety hazards is reduced or minimised.

Histogram: A graph which shows distribution of light in an image.

House style: A business or product brand's preferred design style for visual material, including colours, font styles or typeface.

Image editing software: A computer program used to edit digital graphics.

Industry standard: An agreed set of rules between businesses in a similar industry, such as design or construction.

Key light: The main source of light used in a frame to light the subject.

Layer styles: Editable effects that can be applied to images to add extra features.

Layout conventions: Standard key terms used to label different parts of a graphical product.

Licence: Officially allowing someone permission to use certain assets.

Logo: A shape or symbol used by a brand so consumers can easily identify them.

Lossless: An image that does not lose any quality at all when reduced.

Lossy: An image that will lose some of its original quality when it is reduced.

Margins: The space from the edge of a canvas which helps frame the canvas and provides a guide for the different graphical elements to be placed on it.

Media codes: Tools and techniques used to construct meaning in media products.

Media industry: The companies, organisations and individuals that plan, design, create and distribute media products.

Metaphor: Where an object is referred to directly as something that it is not.

Milestone: A significant or important stage in the development of a project.

Mind map: A diagram used to organise information in a visual way. A central idea is placed in the middle, key ideas arranged around this and the associated points for each idea arranged around them.

Mood board: A physical or digital collage which visually represents a certain style, look or tone for a media product using images, text, colours, fonts, materials and textures.

Node: A shape in a diagram that contains information and has lines running to or from it which connect further information to it.

Non-commercial: The asset would not be allowed to be used to make money, such as for personal and educational use.

Opacity: How transparent or solid an image is.

Permission: The content creator allowing somebody else to use their assets.

Pixel: A tiny square of information/data that makes up a digital image.

Pixel dimension: The vertical and horizontal unit measurements of an image. Usually in inches or centimetres.

Pixels per inch (PPI): The number of pixels in a single square inch of the canvas in a digital graphic.

Platform: A technology that has been designed and built to deliver specific media products or content to audiences.

Post-production: Any work done or changes made to a media product after filming or recording has taken place.

Pre-production: The phase where ideas are developed, and media products are planned.

Primary research methods: First-hand accounts, data and opinions collected specifically for the project, product or idea.

Primary resources: An original source of information about a topic.

Production: The phase at which media products are created, assembled and finalised.

Prototype: A practice model of a product on which the final product can be based which is used to test and improve the concept.

Qualitative: Research based on the quality of data received, rather than the quantity.

Quantitative: Data that is based on numbers and the quantity of responses.

Raster/bitmap image: A type of image that uses pixels to create images.

Rasterised: The process of making a vector image into a bitmap/raster graphic.

Resampled: Where the number of pixels is changed to a different value.

Resolution: The level of detail that is held in an image that affects how clear it is.

Resources: Any item necessary to accomplish a task or carry out an activity.

Retouch: Editing digital graphics to remove minor defects in images.

Risk assessment: A document that lists potential hazards, or risks of something going wrong, and puts in place steps to try and lower the chance of them happening.

Sample rate: The number of pieces of sound data that have been captured per second.

Scalable: The ability to make a graphic smaller or larger.

Secondary research sources: Information that has been previously collected and published.

Secondary resources: A source of information created after the fact by someone who was not there at the time and does not have first-hand experience of the topic or event.

Segmentation: A way of breaking down an audience into manageable groups.

Share alike: If the asset is to be shared again, it must be shared with the same conditions as the original asset.

Shooting script: A version of the script that is used in production. It contains camera shots and angles, scene numbers, revisions and amendments and is used by the cast and crew during the production stage.

Slogan: A catchy and short phrase used by a brand which is recognisable to consumers.

Target audience: A group of people at which a product is aimed; broken down into categories such as age, gender, ethnicity, lifestyle and geographic location.

Technical compatibility: The process of ensuring an image is usable for its final purpose.

Technological convergence: Where previously unrelated media technologies come together on the same device/platform.

Timescale: The length of time available to complete a project, task or activity.

Transparency: How easy it is to see through something. If part of an image has full transparency it is see-through.

Typography: The process of designing fonts and ensuring they are easy to read.

Vector image: A type of image that uses points and paths to create an image.

Vignette: Where the background of an image fades into the main content.

Visual identity: Graphical elements or images that form the look of a brand.

Workflow: A sequence of tasks or activities that need to be undertaken and the order in which they need to happen.

Index